# Multicultural GAMES

## Lorraine Barbarash

Wingate High School
Brooklyn, New York

D1041742

Human Kinetics

## Library of Congress Cataloging-in-Publication Data

Barbarash, Lorraine, 1953-
    Multicultural games / Lorraine Barbarash.
        p.  cm.
    Includes bibliographical references.
    ISBN 0-88011-565-3
    1. Educational games.   2. Multicultural education.   I. Title.
LB1029.G3B33   1997
371.3'97--dc20                                                      96-33062
                                                                        CIP

ISBN: 0-88011-565-3

Globe courtesy of Flaghouse, Inc.

**Acquisitions Editor:** Scott Wikgren; **Developmental Editor:** Holly Gilly; **Assistant Editor:** Chad Johnson; **Editorial Assistant:** Amy Carnes; **Copyeditor:** Bonnie Pettifor; **Proofreader:** Debra Aglaia; **Graphic Artist:** Denise Lowry; **Graphic Designer:** Judy Henderson; **Cover Designer:** Jack Davis; **Photographer (cover):** Wilmer Zehr; **Illustrators:** Jennifer Delmotte and Mary Yemma Long;  **Printer:** United Graphics

Human Kinetics books are available at special discounts for bulk purchase. Special editions or book excerpts can also be created to specification. For details, contact the Special Sales Manager at Human Kinetics.

Printed in the United States of America        10   9   8   7   6   5

**Human Kinetics**
Web site: www.humankinetics.com

*United States:* Human Kinetics, P.O. Box 5076, Champaign, IL 61825-5076
800-747-4457
e-mail: humank@hkusa.com

*Canada:* Human Kinetics, 475 Devonshire Road, Unit 100, Windsor, ON N8Y 2L5
800-465-7301 (in Canada only)
e-mail: hkcan@mnsi.net

*Europe:* Human Kinetics, P.O. Box IW14, Leeds LS16 6TR, United Kingdom
+44 (0) 113 278 1708
e-mail: humank@hkeurope.com

*Australia:* Human Kinetics, 57A Price Avenue, Lower Mitcham, South Australia 5062
08 8277 1555
e-mail: liahka@senet.com.au

*New Zealand:* Human Kinetics, P.O. Box 105-231, Auckland Central
09-309-1890
e-mail: hkp@ihug.co.nz

# CONTENTS

# CONTENTS

v

CONTENTS

# PREFACE

Changes in attitudes about culture require changes in our approach to education. Schools, camps, and youth groups need to reflect on the diversity of the ethnic, racial, and cultural makeup of the city or town they're located in. It is important to touch upon each child's background through course work and activities throughout the school year. Children need to learn about, appreciate, and experience their own and others' cultures. A good way to explore other cultures and to learn more about one's own is through play. Each child must learn to be comfortable with himself, yet able to function in society. A multicultural, multiethnic approach to education provides children with information they can use to form opinions and practices for their own lives. Facts can destroy discriminatory and racial barriers. Indeed, better racial and ethnic understanding can be a direct result of wider cultural awareness. The most logical forum for offering multicultural information is in schools and youth groups. The multicultural, multiethnic activities in *Multicultural Games* will help both teachers and youth group leaders guide children in their quests for both self-identity and understanding of how they fit into the mosaic of society.

I developed *Multicultural Games* through many years of camping and teaching experience at the elementary, middle, and high school levels. Although most games are most appropriate for elementary and middle school children, physical educators, youth group and recreation leaders, and classroom teachers will find activities for small and large groups of children from five years old through adults. The 75 games come from 43 countries or cultures on 6 continents. You can conduct all of the games with common gymnasium equipment. Some games may seem similar to others from other countries because they share common traits. Indeed, these similarities indicate that children the world over share common interests no matter their birthplaces.

The success of any activity depends both on planning the activity thoughtfully and on preparing the necessary equipment and supplies. Therefore, I've structured the book to help you be prepared. I provide all the information you'll need to play the games as well as exploration activities to help children discover the cultures from which the games originated. See the introduction for more about how I set up each game page. Also in the introduction, I discuss the national standards for physical education as they apply to multicultural awareness for elementary and middle school children. Moreover, I provide ideas for how you can use the games in this book to develop an interdisciplinary program with other teachers or group leaders to help students become more aware of other cultures across the curriculum. As the game leader, your enthusiasm will make or break the activity. Create an exciting atmosphere where children want to jump in, participate, and enjoy.

To Randy,
My constant supporter and best friend

# INTRODUCTION

Value lies in playing games just for the sake of playing games. Sometimes it's okay to have no other motive than fun, especially in camp or recreation settings. But sometimes it's necessary to use fun as a means to an end. In *Multicultural Games,* I give you a wealth of raw material for either approach. But first, I give you some suggestions for how you can use this raw material to help children develop an awareness and appreciation for the different cultures they encounter in their lives. I start by describing how I set up the games, then I describe how *Multicultural Games* can help educators meet the content standard for multicultural awareness developed by the National Association for Sport and Physical Education (NASPE, 1995). I describe ideas for assessing student achievement, and finally, I suggest ways you can use the games in this book as part of an interdisciplinary approach to understanding other cultures across the curriculum.

## HOW TO USE THIS BOOK

To make planning easier for you, I present every activity page following a "cookbook" approach, setting up each page in the following manner:

## NAME OF GAME

Where possible, I give the name that the game is known by in the country of origin, providing an English translation in many cases.

▶ ORIGIN: I list the country or group most often credited with the origin of the game.

▶ NUMBER OF PARTICIPANTS: I indicate the optimal number for the activity to run easily and smoothly. You can increase or decrease the number according to your needs and the ability of your participants.

▶ AGE: I list the ages of the children who most commonly play the game, but you will have to decide if the activity fits your group's needs and interests, regardless of age.

▶ **GROSS MOTOR RATING:** This listing of the level of gross motor involvement required allows you to choose a game based on the level of activity you desire. Games are rated low, medium, or high. The gross motor rating is determined by the amount of physical exertion required to play the game. A game which requires sustained running, skipping, or jumping is rated high. Games with players waiting in line or a game with short periods of physical activity is rated low.

▶ **COMPETITION LEVEL:** For each game, I rate the level of competition as low, medium, or high. To ensure that your program is well-balanced, take care to include activities of all levels of competition when planning. The competition level is determined by the intensity of the activity. Games which build to an apex, where the intensity increases during the playing time, are rated high. Games without clear, declared winners or games where the playing time is short or the activity is repeated several times during a playing period, are rated low.

▶ **AREA:** Every camp, park, or school has different facilities. Choose the location in your setting where you feel you can best conduct the activity, always making safety your main concern. Prior to any event, check the area you selected for hazards.

▶ **EQUIPMENT:** I list the optimal equipment for each activity. You may need to modify the equipment according to the number of children involved, the special needs of the children, and the equipment readily available. In many cases, I modify the traditional game equipment both to utilize common modern-day equipment and to eliminate sharp or other dangerous items. Where possible, however, I also include a list of the materials you need to construct the equipment used for playing the game in its original setting.

**HOW TO PLAY:** Whenever possible, I describe the games in the form they were originally played. Since some games contained elements that are not accepted developmentally appropriate practices we adhere to today, I explain the traditional method of play for background, then give adaptations to make the game safer, more inclusive, or more active.

*Adaptations:* The adaptations I list after some games modernize the games, making them more appropriate for today's children and teachers.

Beyond the basic game descriptions, I include the following two elements, which I have designed to help you integrate games across the curriculum:

**DID YOU KNOW?** I include a brief fact relating to the people, culture, or way of life of the country of origin to stimulate questions and discussion.

**CULTURE QUEST** I suggest activities to spark a deeper investigation of the country and people.

Let's help children see life through the eyes of a child in the land the game originated.

## NASPE CONTENT STANDARDS AND BENCHMARKS

The National Association for Sport and Physical Education (1995) developed seven content standards that a physically educated person should achieve during the school career. One of the seven standards requires that a physically educated person "demonstrates understanding and respect for differences among people in physical activity settings" (p. 1). They define the standard as the following:

> The intent of this standard is to develop respect for individual similarities and differences through positive interaction among participants in physical activity. Similarities and differences include characteristics of culture, ethnicity, motor performance, disabilities, physical characteristics (e.g., strength, size, shape), gender, race, and socioeconomic status. Elementary school students begin to recognize individual similarities and differences and participate cooperatively in physical activity with persons of diverse characteristics and backgrounds. High school students are expected to be able to participate with all people, recognize the value of diversity in physical activity, and develop strategies for inclusion of others (pp. 3-4).

NASPE suggests several ways that we can achieve this standard; the philosophy of and games in *Multicultural Games* helps you meet the NASPE guidelines. For example, NASPE states that a second grader should be able to play with others without regard to personal differences such as ethnicity. Fourth graders should begin to develop an awareness of their own and others' cultures: "Activities such as dance/music; creative games; and games from varied cultures, ethnic groups, and countries provide an excellent medium for encouraging students to explore their cultural/ethnic heritage"

(p. 40). Moreover, sixth graders should understand their own cultural heritage and "recognize that their classmates also have a cultural heritage that is important to them" (p. 56). By the eighth grade, students should be able to "recognize the role of physical activity in understanding diversity in modern culture" (p. 71).

NASPE suggests sample benchmarks that you can use to help determine whether your program is meeting the standards grade by grade. For example, second graders should display consideration of others as they play the games. You should notice fourth graders showing respect for people from other cultures and backgrounds and for the "cultural significance they attribute to various games, dances, and physical activities" (p. 41). Sixth graders should demonstrate that they recognize the "role of games, sports, and dance in getting to know and understand others of like and different backgrounds" and "recognize the importance of one's personal heritage" (p. 56). You can use these games to help eighth graders understand the "ways sport and dance influence American culture" (p. 72).

Authentic assessment is an important aspect of all education today; NASPE offers ideas for authentic assessment of student understanding in physical education. Find a wealth of ideas for authentically assessing student learning in the Did You Know? facts and Culture Quest sections of this book, which I have based on NASPE guidelines. An assessment example from NASPE for sixth graders suggests that students report on sports that have origins in other countries, comparing how the sport was originally played and how it is played in this country. Furthermore, students' performances in the games themselves can demonstrate that they have reached the NASPE benchmarks. Eighth graders might identify the minority populations where they live and learn a game native to one of those populations. Fourth graders might do a project to help them explore their own heritage by presenting a game associated with their cultural background.

## APPLICATION AND INTERDISCIPLINARY COOPERATION

You can use a wide variety of methods and strategies to include the cultural awareness component that's become so important in our national standards. For example, use resource materials, such as current magazine articles, holiday publications, or cultural stories to supplement textbooks, thereby highlighting the cultural ties that weave events and groups together. Hold food fairs to give everyone opportunities to taste native dishes. Display native dress on costume days. Discuss holidays, seasons, and special occasions, allowing children to share their home lives and customs. Use games and dances to add unique insight to life in other lands. Children the world over create games using readily available materials, making preparation easier for you. Indeed, while children may be reluctant to taste unfamiliar foods or wear unusual costumes, games are an open, nonthreatening forum in which everyone can participate easily and equally.

Along with the usual sport activities offered in physical education, we must afford children, especially in the younger grades, the opportunity to play games from their culture and their classmates' cultures. Survey parents: They can be a great source of information regarding ethnic, national, and cultural backgrounds. Enlist the cooperation of colleagues to create an interdisciplinary approach that includes physical education, social studies, and language arts. When your students explore a particular region, country, or culture in social studies or read a story in language arts class, let them participate in a game from the region as a natural—and fun—extension of their studies. Every subject, department, and group can work together to make great strides in breaking down the lack of ethnic understanding and tolerance. For example, a social studies class studying South America could cooperate with other departments in the following ways:

**Language arts:** Learn Spanish words and phrases.

**Math:** Explore the currency used in South American countries. Convert the prices of common items to dollars.

**Science:** Find out the food products grown in a particular South American country and how they relate to the weather patterns in the country.

**Geography:** Create topographical maps to learn about the terrain of the country.

**Physical education:** Play games native to the children who live in South America.

**Literature:** Find poetry or short stories about or by authors from South America. Read or dramatize the stories in class.

Use *Multicultural Games* as an important tool for promoting ethnic understanding. The introduction of a particular game can act as a springboard for discussion in the classroom. Examine the equipment used in the native method of play to begin a discussion on the location, raw materials, clothing, and foods enjoyed by the people where the game originated. Integrate geography by finding where the region is located in relation to the class. Many games employ tasks related to daily life or adult activities. Children practice planting, hunting, playing house, cooking, raising children, and other adult tasks in the nonthreatening environment of game play. Several games include native language as a part of the actual game. Have the children research similar words in other languages. For example, how many ways to say "Come on!" or "Get ready!" can they find? Mathematics figures in some games beyond scorekeeping in the forms of counting, rhythms, and other simple math skills.

You, whether you are a teacher or youth group leader, must be prepared to offer information regarding ethnic and cultural backgrounds without clouding the picture with your own beliefs. Become aware of your own feelings and biases. Then, identify common biases connected to cultural groups. Offer information with respect and sensitivity to all, providing information to diffuse biases. Avoid, however, dwelling on the biases connected to one particular group; instead, focus on the life and culture of the people, thereby promoting understanding and tolerance through education.

Today, the population of most schools is truly multicultural, creating a need for cultural awareness that is greater than ever before. Ultimately, multiculturalism promotes individual and group success through education, understanding, and awareness. This is a direct step away from success by assimilation, which society required in the past. When children have greater understanding of other cultures, racial bias and prejudice begin to dissipate. Children who understand how their peers live and how their ancestors lived are more able to interact with people as individuals, rather than as cultural stereotypes. Enjoy *Multicultural Games* in your quest to provide quality multicultural experiences for your children.

# GAMES FROM

# AFRICA

# SPEARING THE DISK

▶ ORIGIN: **ETHIOPIA**

▶ NUMBER OF PARTICIPANTS: 2 TO 10

▶ AGE: 9 AND OLDER

▶ GROSS MOTOR RATING: LOW

▶ COMPETITION LEVEL: LOW

▶ AREA: LARGE OUTDOOR AREA

▶ EQUIPMENT: HULA HOOPS
SMALL BALLS OR STICKS

**HOW TO PLAY:** Each player has an object (ball or stick) to throw. The leader has the hoops. Players form a line, shoulder to shoulder, arm's-length apart, facing the path the rolling hoops will take. When the leader rolls a hoop, each player attempts to throw the object through the moving hoop as it passes. Players who fail to throw their objects through the hoop are eliminated until only one player remains. After the hoop passes everyone, players retrieve their objects.

### *Adaptations:*

1. Award players who throw their objects through the hoop a point. Choose a number to play to before beginning.
2. Choose a person to be the hoop roller at the other end of the line.

**DID YOU KNOW?** A wide variety of animals live in Ethiopia—antelopes, elephants, giraffes, lions, monkeys, and rhinoceroses.

**CULTURE QUEST** What types of land are found in Ethiopia? How is this land different from where you live?

# BOA CONSTRICTOR

▶ ORIGIN: **GHANA AND TOGO**

▶ NUMBER OF PARTICIPANTS: 12 TO 30

▶ AGE: 8 AND OLDER

▶ GROSS MOTOR RATING: HIGH

▶ COMPETITION LEVEL: LOW

▶ AREA: ANY LARGE AREA

▶ EQUIPMENT: CHALK OR CONES TO MARK HOME AREA

**HOW TO PLAY:** Mark the boundaries of a large playing area. Mark an area approximately 10 feet square within the larger area as the snake's home. To begin the game, choose one person to be the snake. The snake chases other players, attempting to tag one. A tagged player joins hands with the snake. Now either player's free hand can tag other players. The newly tagged players join hands with whomever tagged them. If the snake breaks (players drop hands), free players can tag the snake parts. If any part is tagged before the snake can rejoin, this forces the entire snake to return home to reattach all parts. The last free player wins.

A good strategy for the snake to use is to circle the free players, making it easier to tag them.

*Adaptations:*

1. Allow the free players to try to "snap" the snake by running into the joined hands.

**DID YOU KNOW?** Ghana's most important crop is cacao beans, which are used to make chocolate.

**CULTURE QUEST** Bring in a recipe that has chocolate as an ingredient.

# PEBBLE TOSS

▶ ORIGIN: **GUINEA**

▶ NUMBER OF PARTICIPANTS: 6 OR MORE

▶ AGE: 9 AND OLDER

▶ GROSS MOTOR RATING: LOW

▶ COMPETITION LEVEL: LOW

▶ AREA: OUTDOORS

▶ EQUIPMENT: SMALL BALLS, NUTS, OR PEBBLES
LARGE FOOD CAN (NO. 10) OR SMALL
PAIL

**HOW TO PLAY:** Dig a small hole in sand or dirt. All players stand approximately 10 feet from the hole. One at a time each player tries to toss a pebble, small ball, or nut into the hole. The player who throws a pebble into the hole or nearest the hole is the starter and tosses again. If the pebble goes into the hole, the player scores a goal. The player scoring the goal takes a seat near, but not blocking, the hole. The others take turns tossing for a goal. The seated player tosses his pebble at the other players' airborne pebbles, attempting to block shots. When a player scores a goal, he changes places with the seated player. When all players have scored, the game is over. The last scorer becomes the first seated defender in the next game.

## *Adaptations:*

1. Use a large can or pail as a goal instead of a hole. Because you don't have to dig a hole, you may play this adaptation on the grass or pavement.
2. Use a trash barrel and tennis balls instead of pebbles and a hole, pail, or can.

**DID YOU KNOW?** In Guinea, nearly 80 percent of the people work in agriculture.

4

**CULTURE QUEST** Find out what types of crops are grown in Guinea. How are these crops different from the crops grown where you live?

# KUWAKHA NCHUWA
## (TOSSING STONES)

▶ ORIGIN: **MALAWI**

▶ NUMBER OF PARTICIPANTS: 2 TO 10

▶ AGE: 8 AND OLDER

▶ GROSS MOTOR RATING: LOW

▶ COMPETITION LEVEL: LOW

▶ AREA: HARDTOP OR GRASSY AREA

▶ EQUIPMENT: 100 TO 200 SMALL, SMOOTH PEBBLES OF ANY SHAPE

SMALL, ROUND PEBBLE THE SIZE OF A LARGE MARBLE OR SMALL BALL

CHALK

**HOW TO PLAY:** Draw a circle two to three feet across on hardtop or scratch a circle in the dirt. Heap the smooth pebbles in the center of the circle. The players sit around the circle. The first player tosses the round pebble into the air. While the pebble is in the air, the player quickly picks up a smooth pebble from the pile in the circle and catches the tossed pebble in the same hand that is holding the pebble from the pile. If she misses the catch, she returns the smooth pebble to the circle pile. If she catches the round pebble, she lays the smooth pebble by her side. Each player tosses the round pebble 10 times (or another preset number of times), then passes it along to the next player. Players may continue picking up one stone at a time or may increase the number picked up by one stone each turn until they're picking up five at a time. When everyone has had a turn, the player with the most stones collected wins.

*Adaptations:*
1. Make this a more cooperative game by dividing the players into couples or teams and counting the collective score for each couple or team.

6

**DID YOU KNOW?** In Malawi, a person's lineage is determined through the mother instead of the father.

**CULTURE QUEST** Trace your family history back through your great-grandparents. Find out where each family member was born.

# ABUMBUTAN

▶ ORIGIN: **NIGERIA**

▶ NUMBER OF PARTICIPANTS: 6 TO 8

▶ AGE: 6 AND OLDER

▶ GROSS MOTOR RATING: MEDIUM

▶ COMPETITION LEVEL: LOW

▶ AREA: OUTDOOR AREA WITH A SAND OR GRAVEL PILE OR BEACH

▶ EQUIPMENT: SMOOTH STICK, 8 TO 12 INCHES LONG
SANDPILE OR PILE OF GRAVEL

**HOW TO PLAY:** Bury a stick in the sandpile so only four to five inches are sticking out. Players sit in a circle around the sandpile. Normally, the leader decides the order of play for the first round and play continues around the circle with each round beginning with the next person in the circle. In the order decided upon, each player removes a scoop of sand with one hand. When the sandpile around the stick is nearly gone, the players must be very careful. When a player makes the stick fall, he immediately runs from the sandpile area. The other players run to tag the guilty player. When the runner is tagged, he earns a penalty point. Then the players pile the sand around the stick and begin again. When a player earns a predetermined number of penalty points, he is eliminated from the game.

*Adaptations:*
1. If you prefer not to chase the guilty player, you could award a penalty for making the stick fall. You could pour a cup of water over the person's head, you could tickle the person, or ask the person to perform a silly stunt for the entertainment of the group.
2. Set a home base for the running player to flee to. If she reaches home base before being tagged, she avoids earning a penalty point.

**DID YOU KNOW?** The most common forms of recreation in Nigeria are traditional songs, dances, and soccer.

**CULTURE QUEST** If a Nigerian student came to your class, what traditional song or dance that would show your culture might you teach him or her?

# BLINDFOLDED HORSE RACE

▶ ORIGIN: **NIGERIA**

▶ NUMBER OF PARTICIPANTS: 12 OR MORE

▶ AGE: 10 AND OLDER

▶ GROSS MOTOR RATING: HIGH

▶ COMPETITION LEVEL: LOW

▶ AREA: ANY LARGE AREA

▶ EQUIPMENT: BLINDFOLDS
CONES
WHISTLE

**HOW TO PLAY:** Create two or more cone courses depending on the number of pairs playing the game. Pair the players so there is a larger and a smaller player in each pair. Divide the players into equal teams of four to six pairs. Blindfold one member of each pair; this is the "horse." The smaller member of the pair rides piggyback. The rider guides the horse through a cone course with prearranged nonverbal commands, such as tapping the shoulders, turning the shoulders, or squeezing the knees. Run as a footrace for time or as a relay race.

**DID YOU KNOW?** The land in Nigeria varies widely: It includes hot and rainy swamplands, dry and sandy deserts, grassy plains, and tropical rain forests.

**CULTURE QUEST** What areas of the United States might compare with the different types of land in Nigeria? What areas contrast?

# CATCH YOUR TAIL

▶ ORIGIN: **NIGERIA**

▶ NUMBER OF PARTICIPANTS: 12 OR MORE

▶ AGE: 6 AND OLDER

▶ GROSS MOTOR RATING: MEDIUM

▶ COMPETITION LEVEL: LOW

▶ AREA: ANY

▶ EQUIPMENT: HANDKERCHIEFS OR CLOTH SCRAPS

**HOW TO PLAY:** Divide the group into partners. Tuck a handkerchief in the back of the pants or skirt of one partner. The partner with the handkerchief stands behind the other partner, holding the waist of the partner. On the signal to begin, the pairs chase each other, trying to steal handkerchiefs from other pairs without letting go of each other. If partners let go, they must immediately stop chasing until they rejoin themselves. When a pair loses their handkerchief, they move to the sideline. Play continues until only one pair still has their handkerchief. The winner is the last pair with their handkerchief. Pairs can all compete against each other or you can divide the group into two teams, using a different-colored flag for each team.

To ensure fair play, rotate partners every round. Players who were in front should have a turn in the back with a new partner. Accomplish the changes quickly by arranging all players in a double circle before initiating play in each round. To change front and back players, everyone does an about-face; to change partners, the inner circle moves one place to the right.

*Adaptations:*

1. You may want to have a few elastic belts on hand in case any players are wearing dresses without waistbands.

**DID YOU KNOW?** Nigeria has more people than any other African country.

**CULTURE QUEST** Find the population of Nigeria. What U.S. state has a similar population?

# FOUR CHIEFS

▶ ORIGIN: **NIGERIA**

▶ NUMBER OF PARTICIPANTS: 28 OR MORE (DIVISIBLE BY 4)

▶ AGE: 6 AND OLDER

▶ GROSS MOTOR RATING: HIGH

▶ COMPETITION LEVEL: MEDIUM

▶ AREA: ANY 50 BY 100 FOOT AREA

▶ EQUIPMENT: 4 DIFFERENT COLORS OF RIBBONS, BANDS, OR FLAGS, 20 TO 30 OF EACH COLOR

STOPWATCH

WHISTLE

FOUR CHAIRS, STOOLS, OR BOXES

**HOW TO PLAY:** The leader chooses four players to be the chiefs. The chiefs sit on the chairs. The leader chooses two soldiers for each chief. The soldiers hold a supply of ribbons in their team's color. On the signal to begin, the other, unassigned players scatter, trying to avoid being tagged by the soldiers. When a soldier tags a player, she gives a ribbon to the tagged player. The tagged player runs to and sits behind the soldier's chief (as indicated by the color of the ribbon). Continue for a designated time period. When time is up, blow the whistle. All players who have not been tagged sit where they are while the captured players are counted. The chief with the most captured players wins. Be sure to rotate the chiefs and soldiers each round.

## *Adaptations:*

1. When a team gets six captives, or any other preset number of captives, the chief stands on his chair and signals the leader to stop play.
2. Instead of having tagged players sit behind the chief, they could deliver the ribbons to the chiefs and return to the field to try to avoid the soldiers again.

**DID YOU KNOW?** Some of the oldest-known African sculptures, called *terra cotta* figures, have been found in Nigeria.

**CULTURE QUEST** Create a clay figure of a person or make a mask like the Nigerians made for special occasions or ceremonies.

# POISON

▶ **ORIGIN:** **RHODESIA (ZIMBABWE)**

▶ **NUMBER OF PARTICIPANTS:** 8 TO 15

▶ **AGE:** 6 AND OLDER

▶ **GROSS MOTOR RATING:** LOW

▶ **COMPETITION LEVEL:** LOW

▶ **AREA:** ANY

▶ **EQUIPMENT:** CLOTH WITH KNOT TIED IN MIDDLE

**HOW TO PLAY:** All players except one form a large circle around the knotted cloth, leaving several feet between each other. The person chosen as "it" stands in the center of the circle, leaving the knotted cloth resting on the floor. "It" calls a player by name or number to join him in the middle of the circle. When the called player arrives in the center of the circle, both players attempt to snatch the cloth and run outside of the circle, behind the other players before being tagged by the other. It will take several maneuvers, passes, and feints to grab the cloth. If the called player gets back to the circle with the cloth, the same "it" remains. If "it" gets back to the circle with the cloth, the called player becomes "it." Allow only a short period of time for the two players to attempt to snatch the cloth. Start with approximately 30 seconds and adjust the time dependng on the age of the players. If no one grabs the cloth before time is up, return the two players to the circle and call another to the center. Be sure to call all players once before anyone is called twice.

**DID YOU KNOW?** Rhodesia changed its name to Zimbabwe after its independence in 1980.

**CULTURE QUEST** Make a travel poster to advertise the scenic and important places to see in Zimbabwe.

# HOW MANY?

▶ ORIGIN: **TANGANYIKA (TANZANIA)**

▶ NUMBER OF PARTICIPANTS: 3 OR MORE

▶ AGE: 6 AND OLDER

▶ GROSS MOTOR RATING: LOW

▶ COMPETITION LEVEL: LOW

▶ AREA: ANY

▶ EQUIPMENT: A LARGE SUPPLY OF COUNTERS, SUCH AS PEBBLES, CORN KERNELS, BEADS, OR THE LIKE

**HOW TO PLAY:** Each player begins with the same number of counters (15 to 20 pebbles or beads). Be sure the size of the counters is appropriate to the age of the players. (Young children should not use very small counters because they are more apt to put objects in their mouth.) Number the players. Player one secretly chooses 0 to 4 counters to hide in his fist, then asks player number two, "How many?" Player two guesses the number he thinks is hidden. If the guess is correct, the hider gives the counters to the guesser. If the guess is wrong, the guesser pays a 1-counter penalty to the hider. End the game at a prearranged time or when one player has all the counters.

**DID YOU KNOW?** In the 1960s, the countries of Zanzibar and Tanganyika united to form the new country of Tanzania.

**CULTURE QUEST** Find out what countries border Tanzania. Have their names ever changed?

# MY LITTLE BIRD

▶ ORIGIN: **TANGANYIKA (TANZANIA)**

▶ NUMBER OF PARTICIPANTS: 20 OR MORE

▶ AGE: 5 AND OLDER

▶ GROSS MOTOR RATING: HIGH

▶ COMPETITION LEVEL: LOW

▶ AREA: ANY

▶ EQUIPMENT: NONE

**HOW TO PLAY:** The leader stands before the group and says, "My little bird is lively, lively." She then quickly calls out the name of anything she wishes. For example, she might say, "Goats fly." If the thing named can fly, the children flap their arms like they're flying. If the thing can't fly and a player flaps her arms in error, the player is eliminated. The last remaining child wins the game.

*Adaptations:*
1. Use walking objects or rolling objects. If walking things are used, the children could drop to all fours if the thing walks. If rolling things are used, the children could drop to the floor and roll over if the thing rolls.
2. Award a player who commits an error a point. The person with the fewest points at the end of the game wins.

**DID YOU KNOW?** The Serengeti National Park is famous for its millions of large, wild animals.

**CULTURE QUEST** If you went on safari in the Serengeti, what animals would you see?

# GAMES FROM
# EUROPE AND WESTERN ASIA

# HUNTER AND RABBITS

▶ ORIGIN: **BELGIUM**

▶ NUMBER OF PARTICIPANTS: 12 TO 30

▶ AGE: 6 AND OLDER

▶ GROSS MOTOR RATING: HIGH

▶ COMPETITION LEVEL: MEDIUM

▶ AREA: HARDTOP OR GYM

▶ EQUIPMENT: PLAYGROUND BALL

**HOW TO PLAY:** Designate one player as the hunter; the rest of the players are rabbits. The hunter dribbles and bounces the ball around the playing area while chasing the rabbits. When she feels she can hit a rabbit with the ball, she stops dribbling, stands still, and throws. If the hunter hits a rabbit below the waist, the rabbit also becomes a hunter. If the hunter hits a rabbit above the waist, the rabbit remains free and does not become a hunter on that hit. The hunter with the ball continues dribbling. She can stop any time and pass to another hunter. Both hunters can throw the ball at the rabbits. Once there are three or more hunters, allow no further dribbling. The hunters can only pass the ball to each other. Continue until only one rabbit remains. The last remaining rabbit is the winner.

## Adaptations:

1. Begin the game as usual with one hunter. When there are two or more hunters and if the rabbit can catch the thrown ball, the hunter becomes a rabbit.

**DID YOU KNOW?** According to law, all citizens 18 years and older must vote in elections in Belgium.

**CULTURE QUEST** What is the legal voting age where you live? How does a person register to vote?

# NATIONS

▶ ORIGIN: **CZECHOSLOVAKIA**

▶ NUMBER OF PARTICIPANTS: 6 TO 15

▶ AGE: 10 AND OLDER

▶ GROSS MOTOR RATING: MEDIUM

▶ COMPETITION LEVEL: LOW

▶ AREA: A CIRCLE APPROXIMATELY 20 FEET ACROSS

▶ EQUIPMENT: MATERIAL TO MARK THE FIELD
VOLLEYBALL-SIZE SOFT BALL

**HOW TO PLAY:** To begin the game, the players stand around the circle, each with one foot touching the circle. One at a time, each player announces the name of a nation of her own choosing. The leader stands in the center of the circle with the ball positioned at her feet. To start the game, the leader calls out the name of a nation. On that signal, the player whose nation is called runs in, grabs the ball, and yells, "Stop!" While the called nation is running in, all the other nations run away from the circle. On "Stop!" the running nations must all freeze. Then the called nation tries to hit another player below the waist with the ball. Neither player can move the feet to throw or avoid the ball. If the called nation hits a player, the hit player retrieves the ball and tries to hit another player from where she originally stood when she was hit. This continues until someone misses. After a missed throw, the ball is returned to the center, and all players return to the starting circle. The last player to be hit with the ball becomes the leader. If no one is hit with the ball the same leader begins the next round. Give penalty points for breaking rules, for missing when throwing, and for getting hit with the ball. When any player reaches 10 points, start a new game.

## Adaptations:

1. Limit the choice of nations to those in the part of the world the children are studying in social studies or geography.
2. Play without awarding penalty points.

**DID YOU KNOW?** The borders of Czechoslovakia have changed many times in the last century.

**CULTURE QUEST** In recent years, Czechoslovakia has been broken into several smaller countries. Name these countries and draw a map, showing their locations.

# DANISH ROUNDERS

▶ ORIGIN: **DENMARK**

▶ NUMBER OF PARTICIPANTS: 8 TO 20

▶ AGE: 12 AND OLDER

▶ GROSS MOTOR RATING: MEDIUM

▶ COMPETITION LEVEL: MEDIUM

▶ AREA: TENNIS COURT

▶ EQUIPMENT: TENNIS BALL
CHALK TO MARK THE COURT
WIFFLE BALL BAT OR TENNIS RACKET

**HOW TO PLAY:** Divide the group into two teams. Play on a regulation tennis court, removing or capping the poles for safety. Draw a square in each corner to create bases. The "in" team bats and the "out" team fields. The out team has one player on each base, a pitcher standing within a circle 25 to 30 feet from home base, and the rest of the players scattered randomly across the "field" with all players at least 10 feet away from the batter.

The pitcher tosses the ball underhand so the batter can hit it from overhead. After hitting the ball, the batter runs to the first base square. If the batter swings and misses a ball, he can still run if he chooses. After the second swing, the batter must run—even if he swings and misses. Runners already on base may try to advance when a batter hits the ball.

The job of the fielders is to return the ball to the pitcher as fast as possible. When the pitcher has possession of the ball within the pitcher's circle, he yells, "Down!" To be safe when down is called, a runner must have at least one foot touching the base square. Any runner who is between bases is automatically out. (An umpire must help rule.) If a hit ball is caught on the fly, the batter is out, and any runner not touching a base square is out. Runners may try to advance on a fly and are safe as long as they are on a base before the ball is caught. Whether the hit is a fly ball or a grounder, however, runners may advance at their own discretion. Therefore, any number of runners can be on a base at the same time. The only exception is that the batter must run after hitting.

Score one run for each complete trip around the base squares.

If all runners are on base except the batter, the batter bats up to three times to help advance the runners. The batter must run to first base with each hit and the regular rules for outs apply. The turn at bat ends if another player arrives at home base. If after three tries no one has come home to bat, the inning ends.

xxxxxxx   Batting team

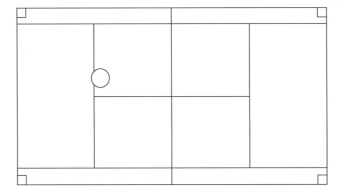

## *Adaptations:*

1. Play for a team score or individual player total. If you are team scoring, ensure that each team bats the same number of innings; if you are scoring individually, keep track of each person's at bats and trips across home base. End innings with three outs for team scoring or when each player has had one or two turns at bat for individual scoring.

**DID YOU KNOW?**  The famous children's story writer Hans Christian Andersen was from Denmark.

**CULTURE QUEST**  Read one of Hans Christian Andersen's stories and design a book cover illustrating the story.

# DREIDEL GAME
## (SPINNING TOP GAME)

▶ **ORIGIN:** **EASTERN EUROPE**

▶ **NUMBER OF PARTICIPANTS:** 2 TO 10

▶ **AGE:** 6 AND OLDER

▶ **GROSS MOTOR RATING:** LOW

▶ **COMPETITION LEVEL:** LOW

▶ **AREA:** ANY

▶ **EQUIPMENT:** FOUR-SIDED TOP WITH STEM
ENAMEL PAINT
PAINTBRUSH
BEADS, CANDIES, OR THE LIKE

**HOW TO PLAY:** The dreidel (draydl) game is traditionally played during the eight days of Hanukkah by Jewish children the world over. It's history dates to biblical times, which is why a particular country is not listed for the origin of the game. The top has letters (*nun, gimel, heh, shin*) painted, one on each of the four sides. These Hebrew letters represent the saying, "Nes Gadol Hayah Sham," which means, "A great miracle occurred there." This refers to the lamp oil that was only enough to light the ceremonial lamp for one night yet stayed lit for eight days.

The players start with an equal number of markers (beads, candies, or the like). Players take turns spinning the dreidel, adding one marker to the pot for each spin of the dreidel. When the dreidel stops, the spinner is awarded as follows:

> *Nun*—get nothing from the pot
> *Gimel*—get the entire pot
> *Heh*—get half the pot
> *Shin*—add another marker to the pot

The game ends when one person has won all the markers or when the participants agree to stop playing.

Paint the words on the dreidel in English or Hebrew.

| Nun | Gimel | Heh | Shin |
|-----|-------|-----|------|
| כ   | ג     | ה   | שׁ   |

The words represented on the dreidel describe the miracle of Hanukkah.

| Gadol | Nes | Hiyah | Sham |
|-------|-----|-------|------|
| Big | Miracle | Happened | There |

**DID YOU KNOW?** The dreidel game is traditionally played during the festival of lights holiday known as *Hanukkah*.

**CULTURE QUEST** Read the story of Hanukkah. How is Hanukkah celebrated?

# CORKSCREW

▶ ORIGIN: **ENGLAND**

▶ NUMBER OF PARTICIPANTS: 8 TO 40

▶ AGE: 10 AND OLDER

▶ GROSS MOTOR RATING: MEDIUM

▶ COMPETITION LEVEL: LOW

▶ AREA: ANY

▶ EQUIPMENT: TWO TO FOUR CONES OR CHAIRS
WHISTLE

**HOW TO PLAY:** Create two to four teams of 4 to 10 members each and have the teams line up 8 to 10 feet apart. The team members stand in single file approximately 4 feet apart, arms at their sides, facing away from a chair or cone. Place the chair or cone as far away as possible at the opposite end of the room directly behind the team line. Number the members of each team, designating the player closest to the cone as player number one. On the whistle, player number one runs a zigzag pattern through all the team members. At the end of the line, the player runs along the line, around the cone, and back into the starting place. While player number one is completing the circuit, number two starts running as soon as number one has passed number three. When number two has passed number four, number three starts running, and so on. In other words, each player begins running when the person behind him has been passed by the person who was in front of him. Many people will be running at the same time. No runner can pass anyone running in front of him. When players reach their own spots after running the whole circuit, they must stand still so others can run around them. Continue until all players have run the circuit and returned to their places. The team who returns to their starting position first wins.

**DID YOU KNOW?** Formal British speech is called "the King's English."

**CULTURE QUEST** What are some common English words that have different meanings in the United States than in Great Britain (e.g., "lift" means elevator)?

# HOPSCOTCH

▶ ORIGIN: **ENGLAND**

▶ NUMBER OF PARTICIPANTS: 2 TO 6

▶ AGE: 5 AND OLDER

▶ GROSS MOTOR RATING: LOW

▶ COMPETITION LEVEL: LOW

▶ AREA: ANY HARDTOP SURFACE

▶ EQUIPMENT: CHALK OR FLOOR TAPE
FLAT STONE OR OTHER MARKER

**HOW TO PLAY:** The game of hopscotch can be traced to England. Many variations of the game exist, but the rules are basically the same for all.

In this version, each player has a small, flat stone to use as a marker. The object of the game is to toss the marker onto the number 1 square, hop on one foot onto the square, kick the marker back over the baseline (using the free foot), and hop back out. If the player accomplishes this, he performs the same sequence with the number 2 square, first hopping onto the number 1 square before hopping on the same foot to the number 2 square. The sequence continues through number 10.

A player's turn is over if

• the other foot touches down when hopping or standing still,
• he hops on a line,
• the stone toss does not land in the correct number square, or
• the kicked stone fails to go over the baseline.

When one player misses, the next player begins from the point the miss happened. The winner is the first player to complete the tossing and kicking sequence from 1 to 10.

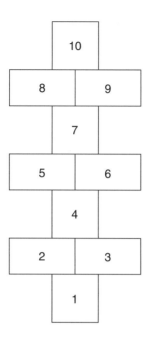

## Adaptations:

1. To make the game longer or more difficult, the player who completes the tossing and kicking sequence back down from 10 to 1 first is the winner.
2. Another popular way to play is to hop on one foot in the single squares and straddle the double squares, placing one foot in each square. The foot in the box kicks the marker.

**DID YOU KNOW?** The British Empire once included land all around the globe.

**CULTURE QUEST** England is only one part of Great Britain. What countries make up Great Britain?

# HUMAN SKITTLES

▶ ORIGIN: **ENGLAND**

▶ NUMBER OF PARTICIPANTS: 3

▶ AGE: 10 AND OLDER

▶ GROSS MOTOR RATING: HIGH

▶ COMPETITION LEVEL: LOW

▶ AREA: ANY

▶ EQUIPMENT: MATERIAL TO MARK PLAYING SURFACE
SOCCER OR PLAYGROUND BALL

**HOW TO PLAY:** This is a dodge ball game for three players. Set up the playing field in the following fashion:

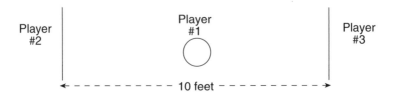

Players 2 and 3 play together to try to hit player one in the legs with the rolled ball. Player 1 can not leave the circle to avoid the ball but can jump or stand on one foot. When player 1's legs are hit by the ball, the player who hit her changes places with her.

### Adaptations:
1. Award points for each successful dodge and for each time a player hits the player in the circle. Rotate players at a preset length of time or number of points.
2. Use soccer-style passes to hit player number 1.

**DID YOU KNOW?** Stonehenge is one of the oldest monuments in England.

**CULTURE QUEST** What monuments would you take a visitor to see where you live?

# ROUND HOPSCOTCH

▶ ORIGIN: **ENGLAND**

▶ NUMBER OF PARTICIPANTS: 2 TO 6

▶ AGE: 5 AND OLDER

▶ GROSS MOTOR RATING: LOW

▶ COMPETITION LEVEL: LOW

▶ AREA: ANY HARDTOP AREA

▶ EQUIPMENT: CHALK OR FLOOR TAPE
SMALL, SMOOTH STONE OR OTHER MARKER

**HOW TO PLAY:** Draw a spiral, marking off boxes.

Player number one hops on one foot, not touching any lines, through the spiral to the rest box. Allow the player to stand on both feet when in the rest box. After a short rest, the player turns and hops around the spiral back to the starting line. If he completes the spiral, in and out, he writes his initials in any box, except the rest box. If playing inside, use cardboard name markers to claim boxes. Player number two begins the same pattern, but can't jump in the initialed box. Only the player whose initials are in a box may

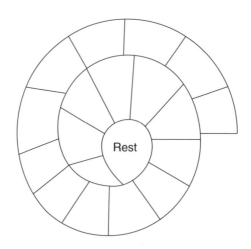

hop in it. Play continues until it is impossible to reach the rest square without missing or hopping in someone else's box. If a player steps in a claimed box or on a line, his turn is over and he is eliminated. The last person remaining is the winner.

### Adaptations:

1. When a player steps in a claimed box or on a line, his turn is over and he does not claim a box that round. This prevents players from being eliminated. The player with the most initialed squares is the winner.

**DID YOU KNOW?** Greater London is one of the largest metropolitan areas in the world.

**CULTURE QUEST** Find out the population of London. What cities where you live are approximately the same size?

# GERMAN HOPSCOTCH

▶ ORIGIN: **GERMANY**

▶ NUMBER OF PARTICIPANTS: 2 TO 6

▶ AGE: 5 AND OLDER

▶ GROSS MOTOR RATING: LOW

▶ COMPETITION LEVEL: LOW

▶ AREA: ANY HARDTOP AREA

▶ EQUIPMENT: CHALK OR FLOOR TAPE
SMALL, FLAT STONE OR OTHER MARKER

**HOW TO PLAY:** German Hopscotch is played much like hopscotch is played in England. The first player stands with her back to the grid and tosses her stone over her shoulder. The box it lands in becomes her "house." If the game is played outside, players may mark houses with initials written in chalk. If playing inside, mark the houses with cardboard name squares. After the house is marked, the player hops on one foot from day to day or number to number, up and down. If her hopping is successful, that is, without missing a box, stepping on a line, or putting the up foot down, the house remains hers for the entire game. Each player tosses, hops, and claims houses in turn. Players may jump only in unclaimed houses or in houses they own. Any player who trespasses on someone else's house while jumping ends the turn. The winner is the last remaining player.

*Adaptations:*

1. When a player trespasses on another player's house, the turn is over. The winner is the player with the most houses when no one is able to jump through the grid without trespassing, touching a line, or putting the up foot down.

**DID YOU KNOW?** The Berlin Wall was built in 1961 to prevent East Germans from fleeing Communist rule.

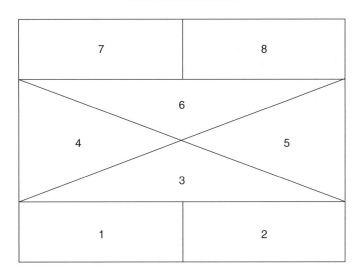

```
          ┌──────────┐
          │          │
          │  Sunday  │
          │          │
┌─────────┼──────────┼──────────┐
│         │          │          │
│ Friday  │ Thursday │ Saturday │
│         │          │          │
└─────────┼──────────┼──────────┘
          │          │
          │ Wednesday│
          │          │
          ├──────────┤
          │          │
          │ Tuesday  │
          │          │
          ├──────────┤
          │          │
          │  Monday  │
          │          │
          └──────────┘
```

CULTURE QUEST Why was the Berlin Wall opened in 1989 after so many years of preventing travel and emigration?

# SCHLAGBALL

▶ ORIGIN: **GERMANY**

▶ NUMBER OF PARTICIPANTS: 12 OR MORE

▶ AGE: 12 AND OLDER

▶ GROSS MOTOR RATING: MEDIUM

▶ COMPETITION LEVEL: MEDIUM

▶ AREA: ANY OPEN AREA

▶ EQUIPMENT: SOFTBALL-SIZE RUBBER PLAYGROUND BALL

CONE OR BASE

BASEBALL BAT

**HOW TO PLAY:** Divide the group into two teams. The batter tosses the ball up in the air and hits it (called *fungo*-style) and runs to the goal (base), 30 to 40 feet away. The fielders retrieve the ball and throw it at the runner. If the runner makes it to the goal without being hit, she scores one point. If she is hit, the other team is up to bat. Do not allow throwers to throw the ball at a runner's head; if a runner is hit in the head, her team does not relinquish the bat.

Keep a batting order to ensure everyone gets a turn. Determine the time or innings you'll play before the game begins.

*Adaptations:*

1. Score runs individually instead of by team.
2. Use a batting tee for younger players instead of hitting the ball fungo-style.
3. Measure the distance from the batter to the base according to the age and ability of the players. Younger players will require a closer base of perhaps 20 to 25 feet.

**DID YOU KNOW?** Germans are well-known for their good food, wine, and beer.

**CULTURE QUEST** What foods might be served at a German meal? Look up a recipe and prepare German food to share.

# GREEK BALL GAME

▶ ORIGIN: **GREECE**

▶ NUMBER OF PARTICIPANTS: 20 TO 30

▶ AGE: 9 AND OLDER

▶ GROSS MOTOR RATING: MEDIUM

▶ COMPETITION LEVEL: MEDIUM

▶ AREA: ANY LARGE AREA

▶ EQUIPMENT: PLAYGROUND BALL OR VOLLEYBALL
WHISTLE
MATERIAL TO MARK THE PLAYING FIELD

**HOW TO PLAY:** Divide the group into two teams. Mark two lines 20 to 30 feet apart. Place the ball in the center. Assign each player a number, beginning with "one" on each team. On the whistle, call out a number. The player from each team with that number runs for the ball. The first one to the ball picks it up and freezes. He then tries to throw the ball over the opposing team line. Allow only one step forward when throwing—no more. If the ball goes over the team line, the player scores a point for his team. If the player misses or the opposing team catches or blocks the throw, he does not score. Continue calling numbers until everyone has been called at least once.

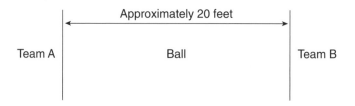

You may want to choose a number to play to or set a time limit before beginning the game. The team who scores the most points in the allotted playing time or reaches the preset number of points first wins.

*Adaptations:*

1. Adjust the distance between lines according to the ages and throwing abilities of the players.

**DID YOU KNOW?** All major European alphabets are based on the ancient Greek alphabet.

**CULTURE QUEST** Look up the Greek alphabet and write a message to a friend using the Greek letters.

# SKYROS

▶ **ORIGIN:** **GREECE**

▶ **NUMBER OF PARTICIPANTS:** 20 TO 30

▶ **AGE:** 10 AND OLDER

▶ **GROSS MOTOR RATING:** HIGH

▶ **COMPETITION LEVEL:** MEDIUM

▶ **AREA:** HARDTOP OR GRASSY AREA

▶ **EQUIPMENT:** PLAYGROUND BALL OR VOLLEYBALL
TAPE OR CHALK TO MARK COURT
WHISTLE
PINNIES OR COLORED T-SHIRTS

**HOW TO PLAY:** Divide the group into two teams. Mark off two baselines approximately 75 feet apart and a middle line halfway between the base lines. Line up the teams on opposite baselines. On the signal to begin, all players rush to get the ball, which was placed on the middle line. The object of the game is to move the ball down the field and over the other team's baseline. The only way the players may move the ball is by passing—no dribbling or running. A player must intercept the ball during a pass in order for it to change team possession—no pushing other players or grabbing the

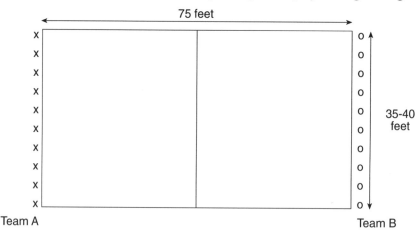

ball from a player's hands. Each time the ball is passed to a teammate behind the opposing baseline, a point is scored. Following a point, the teams line up on their starting baselines and begin as before. Use a referee to monitor the action, especially the level of body contact.

**DID YOU KNOW?** Children in Ancient Greece played with dolls, tops, dice, and board games.

**CULTURE QUEST** The Olympics began in Ancient Greece. When did the first Olympics take place? What events were held?

# TRIANGLE GAME

▶ ORIGIN: **GREECE**

▶ NUMBER OF PARTICIPANTS: 2 TO 6

▶ AGE: 6 AND OLDER

▶ GROSS MOTOR RATING: LOW

▶ COMPETITION LEVEL: LOW

▶ AREA: HARDTOP

▶ EQUIPMENT: CHALK

SMALL, COLORED STONES OR OTHER MARKERS (A DIFFERENT COLOR FOR EACH PLAYER)

**HOW TO PLAY:** Draw this diagram on the pavement:

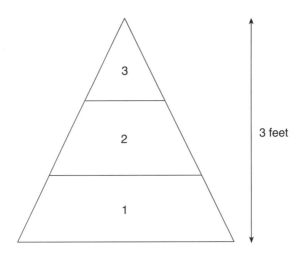

Players, who each have three small, colored stones, stand behind a line, 10 to 15 feet from the base of the triangle. They may take turns tossing or toss all three stones, one at a time, in one turn. Stones may be knocked out of the triangle or into another section by other stones. When the players have tossed all the stones, they total their scores. Stones count for one, two, or three points, depending upon which sections of the triangle they landed in. Stones on the line earn the lower points. (The stone must be *completely* inside an area for the higher points to count.) Play rounds until one player reaches 50 points.

**DID YOU KNOW?** No part of Greece is more than 85 miles from the sea.

**CULTURE QUEST** Greece has many famous landmarks. Write a short story that includes one of them as part of the story.

# GIOCO DEL MONDO
## (ITALIAN HOPSCOTCH)

▶ ORIGIN: **ITALY**

▶ NUMBER OF PARTICIPANTS: 2 TO 6

▶ AGE: 6 AND OLDER

▶ GROSS MOTOR RATING: LOW

▶ COMPETITION LEVEL: LOW

▶ AREA: FLAT PAVEMENT OR FLOOR

▶ EQUIPMENT: CHALK OR FLOOR TAPE
MARKER (SMOOTH STONE OR THE LIKE)

**HOW TO PLAY:** Using the chalk, draw this diagram:

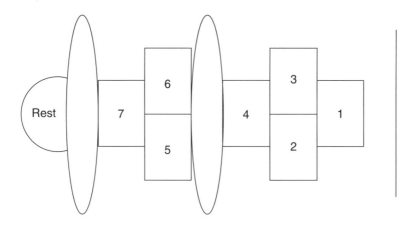

One player at a time takes a turn tossing a stone onto the diagram from a distance of approximately three feet. The stone must land on space number 1 in order for the player to begin. Players hop and straddle through the diagram, skipping over the blank ovals. (Hop on one foot on numbers 1, 4, and 7 and straddle with one foot in each square for numbers 2 and 3 and 5 and 6.) When the player reaches the rest space, he jumps, simultaneously turning around, then returns down the numbers. On the return trip, the player stops one number before the marked number, bends and picks up the marker without the other foot touching the ground, then continues jumping. This completes a player's turn. If a player fails to complete the turn properly, on his next turn he again tosses to the number 1 space. If he completes the turn, he tosses to the number 2 space on his next turn. Play continues in this manner through number 7.

The stone must land within the correct number space for the player to take a turn. If the stone does not land on the correct number space, the next player tosses. If the stone lands on the blank oval between spaces 4 and 5 and 6, the player loses a turn. If it lands on the blank oval between 7 and rest, the player starts over at number 1.

### Adaptations:

1. Play the game with the players skipping the square the marker is on.

**DID YOU KNOW?** Italy is famous for its pasta.

**CULTURE QUEST** What's your favorite pasta dish? Name and draw 15 pasta shapes.

# PEPPERCHES

▶ ORIGIN: **LUXEMBOURG**

▶ NUMBER OF PARTICIPANTS: 5 TO 10

▶ AGE: 8 AND OLDER

▶ GROSS MOTOR RATING: MEDIUM

▶ COMPETITION LEVEL: LOW

▶ AREA: ANY AREA WITH A WALL ON ONE END

▶ EQUIPMENT: SMALL, SOFT RUBBER BALL

**HOW TO PLAY:** All players stand in a line about eight feet from the wall. Designate a player to toss the ball against the wall using an underhand motion, making the ball take a hard bounce off the wall. While tossing it, the player calls out the name of another player. On the toss, all players—except the one called—run away from the wall while the called player collects the ball. When the called player gets the ball, she yells, "Stop!" Everyone must stop running and hold their arms overhead, forming hoops with their fingers joined together. All players must remain completely still—no evasive moves allowed. The player with the ball takes three steps toward a player and tries to toss the ball underhand through that player's hoop. If the ball goes through the hoop, the target player earns a penalty point. Then the scored-on player throws the ball against the wall. But if the tosser fails to get the ball through the hoop, she earns a penalty point. Then, she throws the ball against the wall again to start the next round. At the end of the allotted time, the player with the fewest points wins.

### *Adaptations:*

1. Play to a preset number of points, starting a new game when it is reached. Alter the number of steps the tosser can take, depending upon the ages and abilities of the players.

**DID YOU KNOW?** Luxembourg is one of the world's most industrialized countries.

**CULTURE QUEST** Find out what products are made in Luxembourg. Are any of the products made in Luxembourg something you use often?

# GOELLKI

▶ ORIGIN: **RUSSIA**

▶ NUMBER OF PARTICIPANTS: 11 TO 41 (MUST BE AN ODD NUMBER)

▶ AGE: 8 AND OLDER

▶ GROSS MOTOR RATING: LOW

▶ COMPETITION LEVEL: LOW

▶ AREA: ANY

▶ EQUIPMENT: NONE

**HOW TO PLAY:** This game requires an odd number of players. Designate one person as "it." The remainder of the players form a double line. "It" stands three to five feet behind the last pair in line. He shouts, "Go!" The last pair in line splits and runs to the front of the line, one on each side of the line. They try to reach the front of the line and join hands before "it" tags either one of them. If the couple is successful, "it" returns to the back of the line. If "it" tags a runner, the tagged runner becomes "it" and the old "it" joins the front of the line as part of the chased couple. Caution the players in line to stand still while others are running.

**DID YOU KNOW?** The basic unit of money in Russia is the ruble.

**CULTURE QUEST** Find out how much a ruble is worth compared to your money. How many rubles would it cost to see a movie where you live?

# RIBAKI
## (FISHERMEN)

▶ ORIGIN: **RUSSIA**

▶ NUMBER OF PARTICIPANTS: 5 TO 20

▶ AGE: 5 AND OLDER

▶ GROSS MOTOR RATING: MEDIUM

▶ COMPETITION LEVEL: LOW

▶ AREA: ANY

▶ EQUIPMENT: HEAVY STRING

CORRUGATED CARDBOARD CUT INTO THE SHAPE OF FISH

FELT TIP MARKERS OR CRAYONS

HOLE PUNCHER

SCISSORS

**HOW TO PLAY:** Each child decorates a fish using the markers or crayons. Attach a long string from a hole punched in the front of the fish. Tuck the end of the string of the fish into the back of each child's pants or skirt. Be sure the fish drag behind the players on the floor. On the signal to begin, players attempt to step on the other players' fish. Players gather the fish they step on. Players who lose their fish leave the playing area until all fish are captured. No one may use the hands at anytime except to pick up the captured fish. The player capturing five fish first wins. Be sure the playing area is clearly marked to prevent players from running too far away.

**DID YOU KNOW?** Russia was only one part of the former Union of Soviet Socialist Republics.

**CULTURE QUEST** What republics made up the former Union of Soviet Socialist Republics?

# SQUARE PULL

▶ ORIGIN: **RUSSIA**

▶ NUMBER OF PARTICIPANTS: 40 TO 80

▶ AGE: 8 AND OLDER

▶ GROSS MOTOR RATING: HIGH

▶ COMPETITION LEVEL: MEDIUM-HIGH

▶ AREA: ANY LARGE AREA

▶ EQUIPMENT: TWO LENGTHS OF HEAVY ROPE, 20 TO 30 FEET LONG

WHISTLE

FOUR CONES

**HOW TO PLAY:** Use both ropes tied in the center to form an X. You may wish to wrap the center X with duct tape for reinforcement. Tie a loop on each of the four ends to form handles. Place a cone two to three yards from each of the four ends, making sure that each cone is the same distance from its end as the others. Divide the group into four equal teams, one team holding on to each section of the ropes. On the whistle, a four-way tug-of-war begins. The player holding the handle tries to reach out and grab the team's cone. The first team to grab the cone wins. You may wish to hang flags on the cones to make them easier to grab.

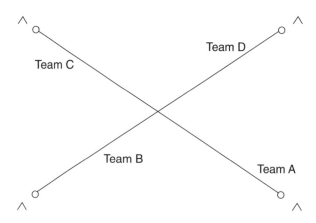

**DID YOU KNOW?** Marius Petipa, a famous Russian ballet choreographer, created the ballets *Sleeping Beauty* and *Swan Lake.*

**CULTURE QUEST** Watch a video recording of *Sleeping Beauty* or *Swan Lake.* Tell the story.

# HALLIHALLO

▶ ORIGIN: **SWITZERLAND**

▶ NUMBER OF PARTICIPANTS: 10 OR MORE

▶ AGE: 9 AND OLDER

▶ GROSS MOTOR RATING: LOW

▶ COMPETITION LEVEL: LOW

▶ AREA: ANY

▶ EQUIPMENT: SOFT RUBBER BALL OR BEANBAG

**HOW TO PLAY:** All players sit in a single line with the leader first in line, holding the ball or beanbag. The leader states a category and letter, having chosen the answer before beginning. For example, the leader might say, "It is a flower beginning with the letter *C*." After the challenge, she hands the ball over her shoulder to the next player in line who then guesses. If the player guesses right, she changes places with the leader. The old leader goes to the end of the line. But if the player guesses incorrectly, she passes the ball back to the next player. The passing continues until someone gets the correct answer. The person who guesses correctly becomes the leader and sits at the front of the line. If no one guesses the correct answer, keep the same challenge category and use the next letter of the alphabet (e.g., a flower beginning with the letter *D*). The same leader chooses the correct answer. Keep the ball moving quickly to keep the game flowing. It is helpful to prepare a list of challenges in advance to secretly share one at a time with each leader.

To prevent the person presenting the challenge from changing the correct answer, have them whisper the solution to the adult leader before stating the challenge aloud.

**DID YOU KNOW?** The main leisure activities in Switzerland include skiing, sledding, camping, and hiking.

**CULTURE QUEST** What are the main leisure activities where you live? Why are they similar or different from the Swiss pastimes?

GAMES FROM

# CENTRAL AND SOUTH AMERICA

# BALON EN EL AIRE
## (BALL IN THE AIR)

▶ ORIGIN: **ARGENTINA**

▶ NUMBER OF PARTICIPANTS: 30 TO 40

▶ AGE: 10 AND OLDER

▶ GROSS MOTOR RATING: HIGH

▶ COMPETITION LEVEL: LOW

▶ AREA: GRASSY AREA OR GYM

▶ EQUIPMENT: VOLLEYBALL OR PLAYGROUND BALL
CONES TO MARK FIELD
WHISTLE
PEN AND PAPER

**HOW TO PLAY:** In an area approximately 80 by 80 feet, arrange the playing area in the following manner:

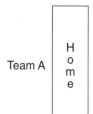

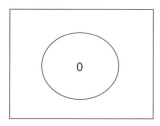

Team B is arranged on the circle.

Divide the group into two teams. Place the ball in the center of team $B$'s circle to begin each round. On the whistle, team $A$ runs around the cones that mark the boundaries of the playing area and back to the home box. They may run in line or in random formation. While team $A$ is running, team $B$ passes the ball backward overhead around the circle, taking turns each round as the one who runs to the center of the circle to get the ball to begin passing it. Make sure every player handles the ball in order, always passing it with both hands—no throwing. When all members of team *A* are back in the home box, they yell, "Stop!" in Spanish: *"Parar!"* When team *A* yells, *"Parar!"* team *B* freezes and stops passing the ball. The leader counts the number of completed ball passes and records it. The teams switch places and repeat the activity after each run or after a preset number of runs. Continue playing for as many rounds as you wish. At the end of the playing time, the team with the highest total wins.

### *Adaptations:*

1. Arrange team *B* so they face outward from the circle. Pass the ball sideways from person to person, each person still handling the ball with both hands.
2. Pass the ball through the legs to the player behind.
3. Change the method of locomotion used by the running team: skip, gallop, slide, holding hands in pairs, and the like.

**DID YOU KNOW?** Soccer is the favorite sport in Argentina.

**CULTURE QUEST** What places in Argentina would be interesting to visit on a vacation? Why would you like to go there?

# PETECA

▶ ORIGIN: **BRAZIL**

▶ NUMBER OF PARTICIPANTS: ANY NUMBER

▶ AGE: 8 AND OLDER

▶ GROSS MOTOR RATING: MEDIUM

▶ COMPETITION LEVEL: LOW

▶ AREA: ANY

▶ EQUIPMENT: PETECA OR BADMINTON SHUTTLECOCK

**HOW TO PLAY:** In the original game, the *peteca* was made from a piece of leather cut and sewn into a cone shape. The cone was filled with sand until it was tennis ball size. The upper end had several long feathers inserted and the cone was tied firmly closed. For the modern day game, use a badminton shuttlecock for the peteca. Standing in a circle, the players toss the peteca into the air and keep it aloft by striking it with the palm of one hand. Players take turns hitting it to the player next to them, proceeding in order around the circle. They must always strike the peteca upward so it can be played by the next player. Often the players call out the alphabet or numbers as they are striking the peteca. When it falls to the ground, play starts over, beginning with the player who last hit the peteca.

## *Adaptations:*

1. Allow the peteca to be hit by any player in a random pattern instead of hitting in order around a circle. For this version, players stand in a random arrangement.
2. Form several circles and see which circle can keep the peteca in the air the longest. The team with the most hits wins the round.

**DID YOU KNOW?** Brazil has some of the largest rain forests in the world in its Amazon region.

**CULTURE QUEST** How long is the Amazon River? How does it compare with a river near where you live?

# CHUECA
## (TWISTED)

▶ ORIGIN: **CHILE**

▶ NUMBER OF PARTICIPANTS: 20 OR MORE

▶ AGE: 12 AND OLDER

▶ GROSS MOTOR RATING: HIGH

▶ COMPETITION LEVEL: HIGH

▶ AREA: GYMNASIUM OR HARD COURT (OUTDOORS)

▶ EQUIPMENT: HOCKEY STICKS
RUBBER HOCKEY BALL
PINNIES OR COLORED T-SHIRTS

**HOW TO PLAY:** Divide the players into two teams. The teams stand facing each other along the sides of the playing area. Mark a goal line at one end of the field and a "hole" (circle) approximately 3 feet in diameter in the center of the field between the two lines of players. Place the ball in the center of the hole. On the signal to begin, a player from each team comes to the hole and tries to knock the ball from the hole. The one who gets the ball from the hole starts driving toward the goal with teammates joining in to

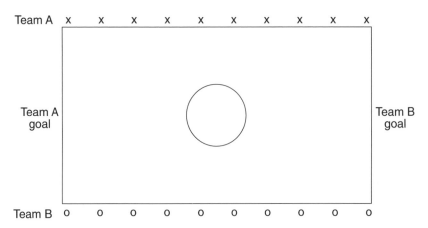

help. At the same time, the opponent's team tries to intercept the ball and score themselves. When one team is successful in getting the ball over the goal line, they score a point, and play resumes with a new face-off at the hole.

### Adaptations:

1. When your players become more skilled, place a goal approximately 4 to 5 feet wide in the center of each goal line. The team is allowed one shot at the goal. If they miss the shot, play is stopped and the ball is returned to the hole. If they are successful a point is scored.

**DID YOU KNOW?** Chileans celebrate their independence from Spain on September 18.

**CULTURE QUEST** Use crayons or markers and paper to make a Chilean flag. What do the colors and the star represent?

# EL PULLMATUN

▶ ORIGIN: **CHILE-ARAUCO PROVINCE INDIANS**

▶ NUMBER OF PARTICIPANTS: 4 TO 30

▶ AGE: 8 AND OLDER

▶ GROSS MOTOR RATING: HIGH

▶ COMPETITION LEVEL: MEDIUM

▶ AREA: GYMNASIUM OR OUTDOORS

▶ EQUIPMENT: LONG ROPE APPROXIMATELY 100 FEET IN LENGTH

SMALL PLAYGROUND BALL

**HOW TO PLAY:** Divide the group into two teams. Make a circle on the ground with the rope. The two teams face each other, standing inside the circle. The object is to roll the ball under one leg and hit a person from the other team. The opposing players try to avoid being hit, but they also try to catch the ball with their hands so they can throw it at the other team. The rolling team scores one point for each opposing player they hit. If a player steps out of bounds—other than to retrieve the ball—subtract one point from that player's team score even if the scoring enters negative numbers. The highest score at the end of the playing time wins.

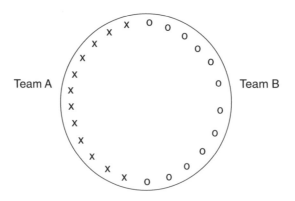

Team A      Team B

**DID YOU KNOW?** The Arauco Indians were farmers and fishermen who lived in the Central Valley region before the 1600s.

**CULTURE QUEST** Find the names of the explorers who invaded the Indians' lands. Where were they from and what were they looking for?

# CINTAS DE COLORES
## (COLORED RIBBONS)

▶ ORIGIN: **COLOMBIA**

▶ NUMBER OF PARTICIPANTS: 10 TO 30

▶ AGE: 8 AND OLDER

▶ GROSS MOTOR RATING: LOW

▶ COMPETITION LEVEL: LOW

▶ AREA: ANY

▶ EQUIPMENT: NONE

**HOW TO PLAY:** One player is chosen as the Angel (*Angel*), another as the Devil (*Diablo*). All the remaining players are "ribbons." While the Angel and the Devil stand away from the circle, the leader whispers to each ribbon what color he will represent. There should be approximately 10 different colors of ribbons. When there are more than 10 players, duplicate colors. The Angel comes into the circle and all ribbons chant, "Angel what do you wish?" (*"Que deseas Angel?"*) The Angel responds, "I wish many colored ribbons." (*"Deseo muchas cintas de colores."*) The leader asks, "What color do you need?" (*"Que color necesitas?"*) The Angel stands in front of a player and names a color. If the color named matches the color the player was given, he stands behind the Angel. The Angel keeps guessing until he misses, then he and all his captured players leave the circle area. When the Angel and his captured players are gone, the Devil comes in. All the ribbons act afraid and cross their fingers. The Devil asks the same questions and follows the same procedure as the Angel. The Angel and the Devil keep switching and guessing until they have guessed all of the colors. The winner has the most captured players standing behind him.

### Adaptations:

1. After the Angel and Diablo capture all the ribbons, they can steal each other's ribbons by guessing colors correctly. The Angel and Diablo take turns going down the opponent's line guessing once for each ribbon

until all ribbons have been guesed at. After each player's color has been guessed at least once, count the number of captured players. The winner is the one with the most ribbons standing behind him.

**DID YOU KNOW?** Colombia is the only South American country with a coast along both the Atlantic and Pacific Oceans.

**CULTURE QUEST** The basic unit of money in Columbia is a peso. What is a peso worth compared to your money? How much would a chocolate bar cost in pesos?

# O.A.

▶ ORIGIN: **GUATEMALA**

▶ NUMBER OF PARTICIPANTS: 5

▶ AGE: 5 AND OLDER

▶ GROSS MOTOR RATING: HIGH

▶ COMPETITION LEVEL: LOW

▶ AREA: SMOOTH AREA WITH A WALL

▶ EQUIPMENT: FIVE TENNIS BALLS OR SMALL PLAY-GROUND BALLS

**HOW TO PLAY:** The five players line up facing a wall that is about six feet away. All five players chant the following together in rhythm, repeating each line three times before reciting the next line. When each player says her line she will bounce the ball against the wall and catch it, following the special instructions when given. When a player misses, she is eliminated until only one player remains.

We bounce our ball . . .
>     Against the wall . . .
>     Without moving . . .
>     Without laughing . . .
>     Without talking . . .
>     On one foot . . .
>     With one hand . . . (throw and catch with the same hand)
>     In front . . . (throw, clap, catch)
>     Behind . . . (throw, clap behind back, catch)
>     Whirlwind . . . (throw, windmill arms, catch)
>     Little horse . . . (throw, raise leg, clap under it, catch)
>     Right now . . . (throw, arms stay extended, catch)
>     Half-turn . . . (throw, half-turn, half-turn back, catch)
>     Full turn . . . (throw, full spin, catch).

**Or chant the same in Spanish:**

*Rebotamos nuestra bolon . . .*
    *en contra de la muralla . . .*
    *sin mover . . .*
    *sin reir . . .*
    *sin hablar . . .*
    *en un pie . . .*
    *con una mano . . .* (throw and catch with the same hand)
    *adelante . . .* (throw, clap, catch)
    *atras . . .* (throw, clap behind back, catch)
    *remolino . . .* (throw, windmill arms, catch)
    *caballito . . .* (throw, raise leg, clap under it, catch)
    *ahora . . .* (throw, arms stay extended, catch)
    *media vuelta . . .* (throw, half-turn, half-turn back, catch)
    *vuelta completa . . .* (throw, full spin, catch).

This finishes the first round. If more than one player finishes successfully, repeat, chanting each line only twice. If after this more than one player remains, repeat the chant, each line once. In the event more than one player still remains, go back to chanting each line three times (then two, then one) and continue until only one player remains. The remaining player is the winner.

### Adaptations:

1. When a player misses, she begins with the next line, but earns a point for the miss. The player with the fewest points wins if no one successfully completes the round or at the end of a preset number of rounds.

**DID YOU KNOW?** The Mayan Indians thrived in Guatemala until the Spanish explorers arrived.

**CULTURE QUEST** The Mayans built many large temples. Draw a picture of a Mayan temple. What was the temple used for?

# BOLAN MALDECIDA
## (POISON BALL)

▶ ORIGIN: **MEXICO**

▶ NUMBER OF PARTICIPANTS: ANY NUMBER OF PAIRS

▶ AGE: 9 AND OLDER

▶ GROSS MOTOR RATING: MEDIUM

▶ COMPETITION LEVEL: LOW

▶ AREA: ANY OPEN AREA

▶ EQUIPMENT: SMALL, SOFT FOAM BALL

**HOW TO PLAY:** Two players stand approximately 12 feet apart. One strikes the ball with the palm of the hand, attempting to hit the body of the opponent. The opponent moves to avoid being hit by the ball. After five tries, the two players change places. The first person to score 20 hits wins.

**DID YOU KNOW?** Rubber balls were first used in South and Central America and then taken to Europe by the explorers.

**CULTURE QUEST** Find out what explorers visited South and Central America. Where were they from? Draw a map that shows the route one of them took from his native country.

# BOLA
## (BALL)

▶ ORIGIN: **PERU**

▶ NUMBER OF PARTICIPANTS: 4 TO 10

▶ AGE: 8 AND OLDER

▶ GROSS MOTOR RATING: LOW

▶ COMPETITION LEVEL: LOW

▶ AREA: GYMNASIUM OR PAVEMENT

▶ EQUIPMENT: BOWLING BALL-SIZE RUBBER BALL
THREE INDIAN CLUBS OR BOWLING PINS

**HOW TO PLAY:** Set up the three pins in a triangle with the head pin toward the players, 25 to 30 feet away from the bowling line. The players roll the ball toward the pins, trying to knock them down. The head pin is worth 12 points and the others are worth 6 points. Players must choose a number of points to play to before the game begins (100 points works well). The first player to reach or pass the preset number wins.

**DID YOU KNOW?** Almost all Peruvians are Roman Catholic and attend annual festivals, called *a feria,* to honor their town's patron saint.

**CULTURE QUEST** Find out what holidays are celebrated in Peru. How do the people celebrate?

# RELOJ
## (CLOCK)

▶ ORIGIN: **PERU**

▶ NUMBER OF PARTICIPANTS: 4 TO 20

▶ AGE: 6 AND OLDER

▶ GROSS MOTOR RATING: MEDIUM

▶ COMPETITION LEVEL: LOW

▶ AREA: ANY WITH HIGH CEILING

▶ EQUIPMENT: LONG JUMP ROPE

**HOW TO PLAY:** Two players turn the rope; the others form a line of jumpers. The object is to give the time, 1 o'clock to 12 o'clock, by running in, jumping the correct number of times, and running out—without missing or getting hit by the rope. After jumping the correct number and running out, the jumper goes to the end of the line. Players continue with the number of jumps, increasing from 1 to 12. If the jumper misses or touches the rope, he changes places with one of the turners. A jumper must run in immediately when it is his turn. Therefore, do not allow rope turns between players. If the jumper hesitates, he changes places with a turner.

**DID YOU KNOW?** The Inca Indians built a great empire in Peru from the 1200s to the 1500s.

**CULTURE QUEST** How are the ways of life different for the whites, *mesitizos*, and the Indians in Peru?

# EL GATO Y EL RATON
## (THE CAT AND THE MOUSE)

▶ ORIGIN: **PUERTO RICO**

▶ NUMBER OF PARTICIPANTS: 10 TO 30

▶ AGE: 5 AND OLDER

▶ GROSS MOTOR RATING: LOW

▶ COMPETITION LEVEL: LOW

▶ AREA: ANY OPEN AREA

▶ EQUIPMENT: NONE

**HOW TO PLAY:** The adult leader names one player as the mouse and one player as the cat. The remainder of the players form a circle holding hands. The mouse begins inside the circle and the cat begins outside. On the signal to begin, the cat runs around the outside of the circle and tries to break the held hands or stoops under the held hands to get inside the circle. When the cat gets inside the circle, the mouse immediately tries to get outside. The members of the circle help the mouse avoid capture. When the cat does catch the mouse, whether inside or outside the circle, the leader chooses a new cat and mouse, and the game begins again. Play until everyone has had a turn being a cat or a mouse or until time is over.

**DID YOU KNOW?** The people in Puerto Rico are U.S. citizens.

**CULTURE QUEST** How did Puerto Rico come to be under the protection of the United States?

# GAMES FROM

# NORTH AMERICA

# HA-GOO

▶ ORIGIN: **ALASKA**

▶ NUMBER OF PARTICIPANTS: 20 OR MORE

▶ AGE: 9 AND OLDER

▶ GROSS MOTOR RATING: LOW

▶ COMPETITION LEVEL: LOW

▶ AREA: ANY

▶ EQUIPMENT: BRIGHTLY COLORED BANNER ON A STICK

**HOW TO PLAY:** The game Ha-Goo was very popular with Thlinget children in southeast Alaska.

The game begins with the players standing in two parallel lines, facing each other 20 to 30 feet apart. A leader from one team (determined before play begins) signals by waving the banner and calling out, *"Ha-Goo!"* meaning, "Come on!" One player from the other team advances. The team with the banner has 20 to 30 seconds to make the advancing player laugh or smile. If the advancing player laughs or smiles—even the littlest bit—she is eliminated and the banner stays with the same team. If she successfully keeps a straight face for the allotted time, she claims the banner and returns to her team with it. The banner is always awarded to the successful team. Continue the game in this manner until one team is left with one person, who is holding the banner. The team holding the banner last wins.

### Adaptations:

1. Play the game for a set time period. The team with the highest number of players at the end of the time period wins.
2. If a player laughs or smiles, he joins the team with the banner. When one person is left on a team and is holding the banner, he is the winner.

**DID YOU KNOW?** Thousands of glaciers fill the valleys and canyons along the south and southeast coastline of Alaska.

**CULTURE QUEST** What types of plants and animals live in Alaska's cold temperatures?

# MUSK OXEN

▶ ORIGIN: **ALASKA**

▶ NUMBER OF PARTICIPANTS: 12 OR MORE

▶ AGE: 9 AND OLDER

▶ GROSS MOTOR RATING: HIGH

▶ COMPETITION LEVEL: MEDIUM

▶ AREA: ANY

▶ EQUIPMENT: FOUR TO SIX SPONGE BALLS OR BLUNT ARROWS

SQUARES OF FABRIC (THE HIDES) 3 TO 4 FEET SQUARE

**HOW TO PLAY:** Musk Oxen helped teach hunting skills. Begin the game with half the players standing in a large circle and the other half scattered in the center of the circle. The oxen in the center of the circle wear scraps of "hide" over their heads and upper body so they can't see. On the signal to begin, the players around the large circle throw the sponge balls or blunt arrows at the oxen. If an ox is hit in the trunk or legs, it is eliminated and sits away from the playing area until the allotted time is over. The oxen must never let go of the hides. When the preset time elapses, count the remaining oxen—the score for the oxen that round. Switch positions, giving the hides to the new team of oxen and repeat as before. Play as many rounds as you wish, then total the scores. The team with the highest score wins.

## *Adaptations:*

1. When an ox is struck in the trunk or legs, he joins the circle but does not throw balls at the other oxen. He cheers for the remaining oxen, trying to give them hints to help them avoid being struck.

74

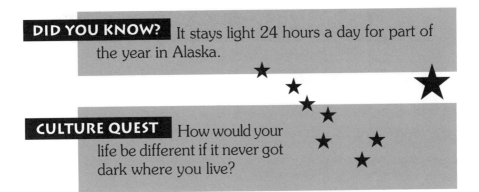

**DID YOU KNOW?** It stays light 24 hours a day for part of the year in Alaska.

**CULTURE QUEST** How would your life be different if it never got dark where you live?

# BOWLING THE MAIKA STONE

▶ ORIGIN: **HAWAII**

▶ NUMBER OF PARTICIPANTS: 2 TO 6

▶ AGE: 12 AND OLDER

▶ GROSS MOTOR RATING: MEDIUM

▶ COMPETITION LEVEL: MEDIUM

▶ AREA: SMOOTH, FLAT AREA

▶ EQUIPMENT: FLAT, ROUND STONES (PATIO FLOOR TYPE)

OR USE

ROUND WOODEN "STONES" APPROXI-MATELY 6 INCHES IN DIAMETER

TWO CONES OR STICKS TO MARK GOAL

**HOW TO PLAY:** During Makahiki, the festival games, bowling the Maika stone was a popular professional sport. A good player could accurately bowl this stone, sometimes made of lava, through a goal 30 to 40 yards away. Some players were accurate up to 100 yards. The maika stones originally used in Hawaii were very heavy and more difficult to bowl than the stones used today.

If you are playing on grass, drive the sticks into the ground 6 to 12 inches apart to create a goal. If you are playing on pavement, arrange the cones to create the goal. Each player takes a turn bowling a stone from a starting line that is 20 to 25 feet from the goal. The player whose stone lands the closest to the goal is awarded 1 point if no other stones go through the goal. All stones rolling through the goal are awarded 3 points. Play to 11 or 21 points.

*Adaptations:*

1. The game may be played in teams, in which case, points for all team members would be cumulative.
2. In any version of the game, determine the distance from the starting line to the goal based on the ages and skill levels of the players.

**DID YOU KNOW?** The Hawaiian alphabet has only 12 letters and every word ends in a vowel.

**CULTURE QUEST** Look up some Hawaiian words. Use the words in a short story about life in Hawaii.

# BAS-QUOITS

▶ ORIGIN: **NORTH AMERICAN INDIAN**

▶ NUMBER OF PARTICIPANTS: 2 TO 4

▶ AGE: 10 AND OLDER

▶ GROSS MOTOR RATING: LOW

▶ COMPETITION LEVEL: LOW

▶ AREA: GRASSY AREA

▶ EQUIPMENT: TWO 16- TO 18-INCH WOODEN PEGS
FOUR 4- TO 5-INCH ROPE RINGS
WHITE ENAMEL PAINT
GREEN ENAMEL PAINT
TWO PAINTBRUSHES
HAMMER

**HOW TO PLAY:** Use stiff rope to construct the rings, taping the ends securely. Paint the rope ring so half the circle is white and half is green. Paint two wooden pegs a bright color so they are highly visible. Hammer the pegs approximately 20 feet apart, leaving at least 12 inches above ground. Each player tosses all four rings one at a time at one of the pegs. The other player stands near the same peg to prevent interference. The second peg is tossed at after retrieving the rings. Toss at one peg, then the other. Take turns tossing the rings. Choose a score to play to (usually 11) or choose a number of rounds to play.

Scoring is as follows:

- Ringer (rope ring fully over the peg) counts as 3 points.
- Leaner (ring leaning on the peg) with green up counts as 2 points.
- Leaner with white up counts as 1 point.
- Any other toss counts as 0 points.

**DID YOU KNOW?** Indians populated every region of North and South America.

**CULTURE QUEST** Create a woven basket or clay pot like those the Indians used.

# BATTLEDORE AND SHUTTLECOCK

▶ ORIGIN: **NORTH AMERICAN INDIAN**

▶ NUMBER OF PARTICIPANTS: 4 TO 12

▶ AGE: 12 AND OLDER

▶ GROSS MOTOR RATING: LOW

▶ COMPETITION LEVEL: LOW

▶ AREA: ANY

▶ EQUIPMENT: HOMEMADE SHUTTLECOCKS: FEATHERS, SEEDS, LEATHER, HIDE STRING

HOMEMADE BATTLEDORES: 9-INCH WOODEN PADDLES

OR USE

TWO OR THREE BADMINTON SHUTTLE-COCKS

PING-PONG PADDLES AS BATTLEDORES

**HOW TO PLAY:** You can easily make the equipment for this game with natural materials. Make a shuttlecock by attaching feathers to a small sack of seeds or to a strong twig. Attach the feathers with a string made of hide or gut. The battledore is a nine-inch board with a wooden handle. The game begins with all players forming a circle, leaving three to four feet between each other. Begin with any player batting the shuttlecock with an under-hand, wrist-up motion to the player on the right. The players must move forward, left, or right to keep the shuttlecock in play—never backward. If a player bats the shuttlecock behind the next player, the batter leaves the circle. If the receiving player misses the shuttlecock or bats it so it can't be played by the next player in the circle, she must leave the circle.

*Adaptations:*
1. As players leave the circle, start a new one. The original circle will keep shrinking and the new circle will keep expanding to accommodate new players. No one is eliminated from the second circle until the first circle

is down to one player. Then begin eliminating players from the second circle. The player remaining in the first circle joins the second circle and the elimination begins again.

**DID YOU KNOW?** Indian homes, food, household items, and crafts reflected the plants and animals native to the area. They traded with other tribes for items they could not grow, gather, or hunt.

**CULTURE QUEST** Choose an Indian tribe. Make a model of a typical home, household object, or ceremonial item.

# CLOWN GAME

▶ **ORIGIN:** **NORTH AMERICAN ZUNI INDIAN**

▶ **NUMBER OF PARTICIPANTS:** 20 OR MORE

▶ **AGE:** 12 AND OLDER

▶ **GROSS MOTOR RATING:** HIGH

▶ **COMPETITION LEVEL:** HIGH

▶ **AREA:** LARGE INDOOR OR OUTDOOR

▶ **EQUIPMENT:** SOFT LEATHER SQUARES ABOUT 10 TO 12 INCHES SQUARE

FIBERFILL OR WOOL

RAWHIDE CORD

OR USE

STRONG CORD, APPROXIMATELY 10 INCHES LONG

SMALL, SOFT BALLS

CONES OR GOALS

**HOW TO PLAY:** This game was played at holiday gatherings when several tribes or clans came together. The Indians lashed poles to form a goal, resembling a football upright or soccer goal. The ball originally used by the Zuni Indians was made of buckskin filled with hair and stitched with rawhide. The string was rawhide or braided fibers. Players marked the ball with a color or design on the buckskin.

To play, place a goal 40 to 50 yards from the starting line. Players begin on the starting line on their backs with their heads toward the goal. Each player hooks the cord with the ball attached over their toes or the toe of one shoe. On the signal to begin, all players kick the foot up and back, flinging the ball and string down the field. After the ball is released, each player jumps up and runs to where the ball landed. After the first fling toward the goal, players kick on their backs at their own pace—not on signal. The first player whose ball goes in or through the goal wins. If a player flings the ball past, not through, the goal, she retrieves her ball, joins the player farthest from the goal, and begins flinging from there.

**Adaptations:**

1. Use cones to mark the goal and small, soft balls instead of making your own.

**DID YOU KNOW?** The Zuni Indians live in New Mexico and Arizona and are part of the Pueblo Indian Nation.

**CULTURE QUEST** Southwestern Indians were excellent weavers. Draw some of their textile or pottery designs.

# DODGE BALL

▶ **ORIGIN:** **NORTH AMERICAN PUEBLO INDIAN**

▶ **NUMBER OF PARTICIPANTS:** 10 TO 30

▶ **AGE:** 9 AND OLDER

▶ **GROSS MOTOR RATING:** MEDIUM

▶ **COMPETITION LEVEL:** MEDIUM

▶ **AREA:** GYMNASIUM OR OUTDOORS

▶ **EQUIPMENT:** SOFT LEATHER OR CLOTH
FIBERFILL OR WOOL
OR USE
A SOFT RUBBER BALL

**HOW TO PLAY:** Divide the group into two teams. The teams line up 12 to 18 feet apart, facing each other. Choose one team to begin with the ball. The first player from the throwing team (team *B*) has the ball. The first player from the other team (team *A*) takes one step forward. The player from team *B* throws the ball at the opposite team's player and tries to hit him. The team *A* player can twist and move to avoid the ball, but may not move his feet. If a player is hit with the ball, he joins team *B*, at the end of their line. If the thrower misses, the thrower joins team *A*, at the end of their line. Continue in the same manner until everyone originally on team *A* has been a target. Then team *A* throws the ball at team *B*. After both teams have thrown the ball, count the number of players on each team. The team with the most players wins.

## Adaptations:

1. Allot a playing time and continue throwing back and forth until the time expires. The team with the most players at the end of the time period wins.

**DID YOU KNOW?** The Pueblo Indians performed many religious ceremonies to promote harmony and order in the universe. They believed if the balance of harmony and order in the universe were maintained, they would have enough food and rain in the coming months.

**CULTURE QUEST** Find out what Pueblo homes looked like. Draw or make a model of a Pueblo town. Why were their homes different from those of many other Indians?

# HANDS AND BONES

▶ **ORIGIN: NORTH AMERICAN BLACKFOOT INDIAN**

▶ **NUMBER OF PARTICIPANTS:** 2 TO 12

▶ **AGE:** 8 AND OLDER

▶ **GROSS MOTOR RATING:** LOW

▶ **COMPETITION LEVEL:** LOW

▶ **AREA:** ANY

▶ **EQUIPMENT:** TWO 6-INCH STICKS
BLACK ENAMEL PAINT
PAINTBRUSH

**HOW TO PLAY:** Hands and Bones was originally played using the long bones of an animal's lower leg. The black ring was painted around one of the bones with natural dyes.

Divide the group into two teams. Teams sit, facing each other. One bone (stick) has a black ring painted on it, the other is plain. A person from one team holds one stick in each hand, concealing the ring. She changes the bones from hand to hand, trying to confuse the other team. The other team tries to guess which hand has the bone with the ring. The player immediately across from the one holding the bones guesses. Award 1 point for each correct guess. Teams take turns holding the bones, and each round a different player holds the bones so everyone has a turn. Play to 10 points.

**DID YOU KNOW?** The Blackfoot Indians lived on the plains in buffalo hide teepees.

**CULTURE QUEST** Find out what other items the Blackfoot Indians made from the buffalo they hunted.

# INDIAN WRESTLING

▶ ORIGIN: **NORTH AMERICAN INDIAN**

▶ NUMBER OF PARTICIPANTS: ANY NUMBER OF PAIRS

▶ AGE: 9 AND OLDER

▶ GROSS MOTOR RATING: HIGH

▶ COMPETITION LEVEL: HIGH

▶ AREA: ANY

▶ EQUIPMENT: NONE

**HOW TO PLAY:** Organize all players into pairs. Each pair stands face to face with their right feet forward and touching sides. The left feet are back in stride position. Then the pair clasps right hands over the touching feet. On the signal to begin, the two try to throw each other off-balance by pushing, pulling, or swinging the clasped hands. Feet must stay in place. To win, a player must make the opponent move either foot.

**DID YOU KNOW?** Some Indian tribes used games to train warriors for combat and to compete for honors.

**CULTURE QUEST** Find the name of a famous American Indian man or woman. What made him or her famous?

# STEALING STICKS

▶ ORIGIN: **NORTH AMERICAN CHOCTAW INDIAN**

▶ NUMBER OF PARTICIPANTS: 2 TO 30

▶ AGE: 6 AND OLDER

▶ GROSS MOTOR RATING: HIGH

▶ COMPETITION LEVEL: MEDIUM

▶ AREA: LARGE OUTDOOR AREA

▶ EQUIPMENT: 10 TO 12 18-INCH STICKS
MATERIAL FOR MARKING FIELD
WHISTLE

**HOW TO PLAY:** Divide the group in two teams. Mark a 30- by 60-foot field in the following manner:

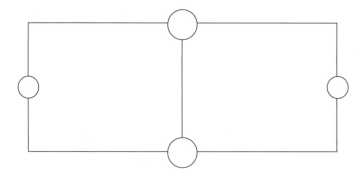

Place several sticks in each of the end line circles. Each circle is four feet in diameter. The circles on either end of the midline are the mush pots, one for each team. Make the mush pot circles large enough for an entire team's players to sit inside. A circle 10 to 12 feet across would work well. On the signal to begin, teams try to steal sticks from each other without getting tagged. The players place captured sticks in their team's end circle. They may be tagged only on the opponent's half of the field. Tagged runners must go to their team's mush pot and remain there until everyone has been captured. Monitor body contact very closely to prevent the game from becoming too physical. The winner is the team with the most sticks in their circle when a team has all been captured or at the end of the allotted time.

### Adaptations:

1. To avoid eliminating players for long periods, each stick captured by a team and successfully placed in their end circle frees all captured players from their mush pot.

**DID YOU KNOW?** In the 1830s, the U.S. government forced the Choctaws to leave their homes in Alabama and Mississippi and march to Oklahoma. The march is called the "Trail of Tears."

**CULTURE QUEST** Why was the Choctaw's march called the "Trail of Tears"? Why did they have to leave their homeland?

# TURN AROUND GAME

▶ ORIGIN: **NORTH AMERICAN INDIAN**

▶ NUMBER OF PARTICIPANTS: 2 TO 8

▶ AGE: 12 AND OLDER

▶ GROSS MOTOR RATING: HIGH

▶ COMPETITION LEVEL: MEDIUM

▶ AREA: ANY

▶ EQUIPMENT: 20 TO 40 6-INCH, THIN STICKS (CHOP-STICKS) FOR EACH PAIR OF PARTNERS

**HOW TO PLAY:** The game was originally a betting game in which treats or trinkets were bet and won. Begin the game with one player holding all the sticks in the palm of one hand. He tosses the sticks into the air. As they fall, the player tries to catch as many sticks as possible on the back of both hands. Put the free sticks aside. Then the player tosses the caught sticks from the back of the hands into the palm. If the player catches an odd number of sticks, he keeps one and repeats the action, using all the other sticks. If the player catches an even number of sticks, the other player has a turn, using all the remaining sticks. The player who catches the last free stick wins all the other player's sticks, and the game begins again.

*Adaptations:*
1. For younger children, catch the tossed sticks in the palm of the hand instead of on the back of the hand. All other rules remain the same.

**DID YOU KNOW?** When Indian boys reached their teens, they had to perform a test of courage and bravery called an initiation ceremony before they were considered adults.

**CULTURE QUEST** What rituals or ceremonies are held where you live that mark the entry to adulthood?

# SKELLY

▶ ORIGIN: **UNITED STATES**

▶ NUMBER OF PARTICIPANTS: 2 TO 6

▶ AGE: 6 AND OLDER

▶ GROSS MOTOR RATING: LOW

▶ COMPETITION LEVEL: LOW

▶ AREA: PAVEMENT OR GYM

▶ EQUIPMENT: SMOOTH STONE, BOTTLE CAP FILLED WITH WAX, OR 1 INCH WIDE WOODEN PIECE FOR EACH PLAYER

**HOW TO PLAY:** Skelly is normally played on the sidewalk or street in New York City, but the game translates well to gym or classroom floors. Make the "checker" for each player of the same material but with different colors or markings so players can easily identify their own. You can paint the skelly grid, draw it with chalk, or outline it with tape on the playing surface. Normally, the grid is the size of a sidewalk block, or approximately four by four feet. The grid has many variations with the following being one of the most common:

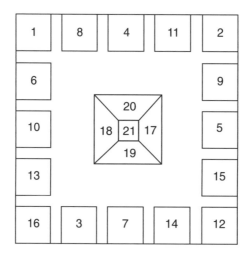

Players decide the order of play before the game begins. The first player pitches her checker from a line approximately three feet from the skelly grid toward number 1. If the checker lands in the number 1 square, she gets another turn. The player continues flicking the checker through the numbers until she is not successful in getting the checker in the next numbered square. If she misses it, she waits until everyone has had a turn and then tries again. If the checker lands in a square, but not the right number, she waits until everyone has had a turn and tries again. After the initial pitch, players move their checkers by flicking them with their index or middle fingers, so players will be playing while on their hands and knees. The spaces in the inner areas between boxes are "skelly." If a checker lands there, the player can't shoot again until someone knocks the checker out of bounds or into a numbered box. Even if only a part of the checker is in skelly or on a line, it is still dead until someone hits it out. The first player to reach the number 21 square and return down the numbers to number 1 wins.

## *Adaptations:*

1. Players may take turns shooting their checkers at the number boxes without using the skelly penalty. In other words, if a player shoots his checker and does not get it in the correct number box, the checker remains where it is until his next turn, rather than waiting for someone else to knock it into a numbered box.
2. Players may take two or three shots per turn. This is especially good for younger or beginning players. If all checkers are in skelly begin the sequence of play again with all players participating.

**DID YOU KNOW?** The U.S. population includes people from virtually every country around the world.

**CULTURE QUEST** Poll the students in your class or group. Where are their ancestors originally from?

# STEAL THE BACON

▶ ORIGIN: **UNITED STATES**

▶ NUMBER OF PARTICIPANTS: 20 TO 30

▶ AGE: 7 AND OLDER

▶ GROSS MOTOR RATING: LOW

▶ COMPETITION LEVEL: LOW

▶ AREA: GYM OR OUTDOOR

▶ EQUIPMENT: INDIAN CLUB OR PLASTIC BOWLING PIN

**HOW TO PLAY:** Divide the players into two teams. The teams line up facing each other, 20 to 30 feet apart. Number the players on both teams so the players with the same numbers are at a diagonal from each other. Place the bowling pin in the center of the open area. The leader calls out a number. The two players with that number run to the pin. Each player tries to grab the pin and run with it back to his team's line without getting tagged by the player from the other team. If the runner makes it back to his line, he scores a point. If his opponent tags him, he does not score. Following each number called out, the leader replaces the pin and calls a new number. Occasionally, the players in the center are reluctant to grab the pin or spend time circling the pin. In this case, the leader may decide to call another number to come to the center to stimulate play. If after a reasonable period of time no one grabs the pin, the leader should instruct the players to return to their lines and calls a new number. The leader must be the only one calling numbers. Play the game for a designated period of time or to a preset score.

## *Adaptations:*

1. Rather than merely calling out numbers at random, call out simple math problems. When the players solve the problem, the players whose numbers are the solution to the problem run out to try for the pin.

**DID YOU KNOW?** Most people think of the Declaration of Independence, signed in 1776, as the beginning of the United States. United States independence, however, was not official until the signing of the Treaty of Paris in 1783.

**CULTURE QUEST** What rights are included in the Declaration of Independence?

# GAMES FROM

# EAST ASIA

# LOO K'BAH ZEE

▶ ORIGIN: **BURMA**

▶ NUMBER OF PARTICIPANTS: 12 OR MORE

▶ AGE: 6 AND OLDER

▶ GROSS MOTOR RATING: MEDIUM

▶ COMPETITION LEVEL: LOW

▶ AREA: ANY

▶ EQUIPMENT: SMALL BALL OR BEANBAG

**HOW TO PLAY:** All players stand in a circle, facing inward with their hands behind them. The person chosen to be "it" walks around the circle and pretends to leave the ball in the hands of each person. When the ball is left in someone's hands, the player who now has the ball tries to leave the circle while the two players positioned next to him try to catch him, but these neighboring players may not leave their spots. If the player with the ball escapes, he becomes the new "it." But if his neighbors catch him, the person who was "it" continues.

**DID YOU KNOW?** The major religion in Burma is Buddhism.

**CULTURE QUEST** What is the eight-fold path that Buddha taught?

# TRAIN STATIONS

▶ ORIGIN: **CEYLON (SRI LANKA)**

▶ NUMBER OF PARTICIPANTS: 10 TO 30

▶ AGE: 10 AND OLDER

▶ GROSS MOTOR RATING: LOW

▶ COMPETITION LEVEL: LOW

▶ AREA: ANY

▶ EQUIPMENT: NONE

**HOW TO PLAY:** This game is normally played using the local train stations in Ceylon. It can be adapted for play with your group by using familiar train stations, towns, or streets.

The group sits in a circle with a leader in the center. Each person in the circle chooses the name of a station. The leader says, "The train runs from _____ to _____." The two people called jump up and run across, trying to switch places. At the same time, the leader tries to beat one of the called players to any of the vacant spots. If the leader gets to the spot first, the player left with no spot becomes the new leader.

If the leader says, "All trains run express!" all players must change places.

*Adaptations:*

1. The leader can call three stations at the same time.

**DID YOU KNOW?** Ceylon is now known as Sri Lanka.

**CULTURE QUEST** When did Ceylon become Sri Lanka? Why did the name change?

99

# CATCHING FISHES IN THE DARK

▶ ORIGIN: **CHINA**

▶ NUMBER OF PARTICIPANTS: 8 TO 20

▶ AGE: 5 AND OLDER

▶ GROSS MOTOR RATING: MEDIUM

▶ COMPETITION LEVEL: LOW

▶ AREA: ANY

▶ EQUIPMENT: BLINDFOLD

**HOW TO PLAY:** Blindfold one player—the fisherman. The rest of the group are fish. The fish run by the fisherman and try to tag him without his tagging them. If the fisherman tags a fish, he tries to guess who it is. If he guesses correctly, then he changes places with the fish. If he guesses incorrectly, the fish goes free. Clearly define the area in which the fish may run.

*Adaptations:*

1. The fish remain stationary and make sounds. The fisherman locates the fish by homing in on the sounds.

**DID YOU KNOW?** China has the world's largest population.

**CULTURE QUEST** Find out the population of China. Compare it to the population of the United States, Russia, and Australia.

# CHINESE CHICKEN

▶ ORIGIN: **CHINA**

▶ NUMBER OF PARTICIPANTS: 10 TO 20

▶ AGE: 9 AND OLDER

▶ GROSS MOTOR RATING: MEDIUM

▶ COMPETITION LEVEL: LOW

▶ AREA: ANY

▶ EQUIPMENT: SHOES, WOODEN BLOCKS, OR BEANBAGS

**HOW TO PLAY:** Divide the group into two teams. In front of each team, place the players' shoes in a straight line, leaving 12 to 18 inches between each shoe. On the signal to start, the first player for each team hops on one foot over each shoe until she reaches the end of the line. At the end of the line of shoes, she uses the uplifted foot to kick the last shoe away, soccer-style. Then she runs and picks up the kicked shoe, runs to the beginning of the shoe line, and places the shoe so the next person can jump over it to start her race. The player can't touch any shoe except the last one on the line. If a player touches a shoe other than the final one, she must go behind it and jump over it again. Continue taking turns jumping and kicking until one team wins by being the first team to have every member complete the task.

**DID YOU KNOW?** English is the most widely studied foreign language in China.

**CULTURE QUEST** Create a menu for a Chinese meal. What ingredients commonly used in China are available where you live?

# CHINESE WALL

▶ ORIGIN: **CHINA**

▶ NUMBER OF PARTICIPANTS: 10 TO 50

▶ AGE: 6 AND OLDER

▶ GROSS MOTOR RATING: HIGH

▶ COMPETITION LEVEL: LOW

▶ AREA: ANY

▶ EQUIPMENT: MATERIAL TO MARK PLAYING SURFACE

**HOW TO PLAY:** Mark the field in the following fashion:

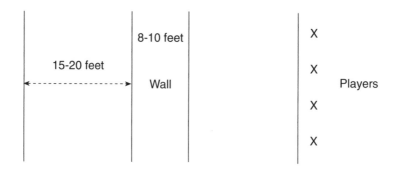

One player acts as the guard on the wall (the center area). The guard may not leave the wall. The remainder of the players stand behind either end line. To begin the game, the guard yells, "Start!" On this signal, all players run to the opposite end line. The guard tries to tag as many players as possible as they cross the wall area. The caught players become guards and join the original guard on the wall. The game continues in the same pattern until the guards have caught everyone. The last person caught becomes the starting guard for the next game.

**DID YOU KNOW?** China has a Communist form of government.

**CULTURE QUEST** How has family life in China changed since the Communists came to power?

# PLANT BEANS, REAP BEANS

▶ ORIGIN: **HONG KONG**

▶ NUMBER OF PARTICIPANTS: 8 TO 20

▶ AGE: 6 AND OLDER

▶ GROSS MOTOR RATING: MEDIUM

▶ COMPETITION LEVEL: LOW

▶ AREA: ANY LARGE AREA

▶ EQUIPMENT: 10 "BEANS" (CHECKERS)
CHALK
WHISTLE

**HOW TO PLAY:** Divide the group into two teams. The first person in each line has five "beans," or checkers. Draw five small circles approximately 20 feet from the lines.

Pile the checkers (beans) at the feet of the first player in each line. On the whistle to begin, the first player runs to the circles and places a checker in one circle. He runs back to the line, grabs another checker and returns to the circles. The same player continues in this manner until he has "planted" all five beans. The next player "reaps" the beans one at a time. Continue until everyone has had a turn planting or reaping. The first team to have all players successfully plant or reap wins.

**DID YOU KNOW?** The British lease on Hong Kong expires in 1997. After 1997, Hong Kong will become a special region of China but will retain the capitalistic society it has now.

**CULTURE QUEST** How did Great Britain come to lease Hong Kong?

# ATYA-PATYA

▶ ORIGIN: **INDIA**

▶ NUMBER OF PARTICIPANTS: 10 TO 20

▶ AGE: 9 AND OLDER

▶ GROSS MOTOR RATING: HIGH

▶ COMPETITION LEVEL: LOW

▶ AREA: TENNIS COURT OR GYM WITH SEVERAL FLOOR LINES

▶ EQUIPMENT: CHALK OR FLOOR TAPE
STOPWATCH
WHISTLE

**HOW TO PLAY:** Divide the group into four teams. Mark off one area of the playing area as a safe area and designate another area as the holding area. One team is the aggressor team, the other three are the prey. The object is for the prey to run along the lines on the floor to the designated safe place without getting tagged by the aggressor team, who is chasing the prey along the lines. The aggressor team and the prey teams may not leave the lines during the chase. The prey teams may begin in one central area or scattered along the lines. Players—prey or aggressors—who leave the lines to avoid capture are automatically sent to the holding area for a one-minute penalty. Tagged players are sent to the holding area where they remain until everyone except one player has been tagged. The game continues until every team has had an opportunity to be the aggressor team.

### Adaptations:

1. A player who is tagged by the aggressors goes to the holding area until a newly captured player from her team arrives to take her place. When a new player arrives in the holding area, the player from the same team who is already there leaves. So, there will be no more than one player from each prey team in the holding area at a time.

2. Predetermine a time limit for the aggressors to chase the prey. Count how many opposing players were caught during the time limit for each team's turn as the aggressors. The aggressor team with the largest number of tagged captives wins.

**DID YOU KNOW?** The chief foods in India are grains, pod vegetables, and fruits since so many people do not eat meat because of their religious beliefs.

**CULTURE QUEST** Find a recipe for a vegetarian dish that uses ingredients commonly found in India.

# FOOT GAME

▶ **ORIGIN:** **INDONESIA**

▶ **NUMBER OF PARTICIPANTS:** 2 OR MORE

▶ **AGE:** 8 AND OLDER

▶ **GROSS MOTOR RATING:** LOW

▶ **COMPETITION LEVEL:** LOW

▶ **AREA:** OUTDOOR AREA

▶ **EQUIPMENT:** SMALL, SMOOTH STONES

**HOW TO PLAY:** The players remove their shoes and choose a stone they can pick up with their toes. Standing at a starting line, players take turns throwing the stone as far as possible with their feet. When all stones have been tossed, the players walk out to their stones and stand where they landed. After retrieving the stones, the player with the shortest toss has to give a piggyback ride to the player with the longest toss back to the starting line. Repeat as long as time allows.

## Adaptations:

1. If the size of the participants does not allow piggybacking, change the penalty for the shortest toss to a more appropriate activity. The player could do a silly dance, crawl back to the starting line, or some other funny activity.

**DID YOU KNOW?** Indonesia is made up of more than 13,600 islands with people living on more than 6,000 of them.

**CULTURE QUEST** What type of traditional clothing do men and women wear in Indonesia?

# RING AND LOOSE ROPE GAME

▶ ORIGIN: **INDONESIA**

▶ NUMBER OF PARTICIPANTS: 10 TO 30

▶ AGE: 6 AND OLDER

▶ GROSS MOTOR RATING: LOW

▶ COMPETITION LEVEL: LOW

▶ AREA: ANY

▶ EQUIPMENT: HEAVY STRING
PLASTIC OR WOODEN RING (E.G., CURTAIN RING)

**HOW TO PLAY:** Thread the string through the small ring and make a large circle with the string. Make sure the circle of string is large enough for all the players to hold it with both hands. The player chosen as "it" stands in the center of the circle while the players around the circle pass the ring along the string. The players do not have to pass the ring with every hand motion; rather, they should try to hide where the ring is from "it." Chant, *"Wora-wora, tjintjin,"* (pronounced, "Wora-wora, chin chin") while passing the ring. Chant faster and faster as the ring moves faster and faster. "It" calls stop after four to six chants. If "it" guesses whose hand is hiding the ring, they change places. If the guess is incorrect, "it" must give a piggyback ride to the accused around the circle.

### Adaptations:

1. If the size of the participants does not allow piggybacking, create a more appropriate stunt.

**DID YOU KNOW?** Indonesians hold ox races and bull fights during festival times.

**CULTURE QUEST** What are the major agricultural products grown in Indonesia?

# BIG LANTERN

▶ ORIGIN: **JAPAN**

▶ NUMBER OF PARTICIPANTS: 10 OR MORE

▶ AGE: 6 AND OLDER

▶ GROSS MOTOR RATING: LOW

▶ COMPETITION LEVEL: LOW

▶ AREA: ANY

▶ EQUIPMENT: NONE

**HOW TO PLAY:** All players sit in a circle on the floor. Designate one player as the leader, who starts by saying, "Little lantern," spreading his hands far apart. The next player says, "Big lantern," placing his hands close together. Continue around the circle, alternating sayings and hand motions. Repeat the chant and hand motions as quickly as possible. Go as quickly as possible to try to confuse players. Eliminate players when they make the wrong hand motion with the saying. The last person in the circle is the winner.

### *Adaptations:*

1. Award the player a point or a letter (B-I-G-L-A-N-T-E-R-N) if the wrong hand motion is given with the words. The person with the fewest points or letters at the end of a preset time period wins.

**DID YOU KNOW?** Fish are the main source of protein in the Japanese diet.

**CULTURE QUEST** Green tea is a common hot beverage in Japan. Have a tea ceremony and serve green tea.

# BOUNCE THE BALL

▶ ORIGIN: **JAPAN**

▶ NUMBER OF PARTICIPANTS: 2 TO 10

▶ AGE: 8 AND OLDER

▶ GROSS MOTOR RATING: LOW

▶ COMPETITION LEVEL: LOW

▶ AREA: HARDTOP OR GYM

▶ EQUIPMENT: PLAYGROUND BALL

**HOW TO PLAY:** One player at a time bounces the ball hard on the floor, spins around once, and faces the ball in time to be watching the first bounce. After the ball bounces for the first time, dribble it five times. After everyone has a try, increase the spins for the round to two, then three, and so on. The dribbles do not increase. If a player is able to complete one spin, she advances to two, then three, and so forth. Only players who successfully complete a round advance to the next round of more spins. If a player is unable to complete the spins and dribbles, she is eliminated. The winner is the player who can complete the highest number of spins.

*Adaptations:*

1. Do not eliminate players who are unable to complete the spins and dribbles. On the next turn, they start on the number they were unable to complete.

**DID YOU KNOW?** Most Japanese people follow the Shinto and Buddhist religions.

**CULTURE QUEST** How do the religious beliefs of the Shintos or Buddhists influence their daily lives?

# JAPANESE TAG

▶ ORIGIN: **JAPAN**

▶ NUMBER OF PARTICIPANTS: 10 TO 30

▶ AGE: 8 AND OLDER

▶ GROSS MOTOR RATING: HIGH

▶ COMPETITION LEVEL: LOW

▶ AREA: ANY LARGE AREA

▶ EQUIPMENT: NONE

**HOW TO PLAY:** Choose one person to be "it." He calls out a position, for example, "Right elbow on left knee," or, "Both hands on the ground." After calling out a few positions, he calls *"Tomare!"* or "Halt!" Players must freeze in the position they were in when halt was called. Eliminate all players who are not in the last called position. The game continues until only one player remains. The remaining player becomes the next "it."

*Adaptations:*

1. The person who tags "it" first changes places with him. Resume the game and repeat the process. This prevents players from being eliminated.

**DID YOU KNOW?** The Japanese islands experience about 1,500 earthquakes of varying strength every year.

**CULTURE QUEST** How have earthquakes influenced building construction in Japan?

# PICK-UP STICKS

▶ ORIGIN: **LAOS**

▶ NUMBER OF PARTICIPANTS: 2 TO 4

▶ AGE: 5 AND OLDER

▶ GROSS MOTOR RATING: LOW

▶ COMPETITION LEVEL: LOW

▶ AREA: ANY LEVEL AREA

▶ EQUIPMENT: 15 TO 30 10-INCH CHOPSTICKS OR SIMILAR STICKS

SMALL BALL OR LARGE NUT

**HOW TO PLAY:** Each pair of players has a bunch (10 to 15) of sticks and a small, round ball or large, round nut (such as a walnut). Hold the sticks five to six inches above the floor and drop the whole bundle. The sticks will fall in a random pattern. Toss the ball up and quickly pick up one stick before catching the ball. If a player successfully catches the ball in the hand holding the stick, the same player continues the next turn. He picks up two sticks on the next attempt, then three, and so on as long as he is successful, each time emptying his hand before trying for more sticks. If a player picks up the wrong number of sticks or fails to catch the ball, his turn is over. The next player then drops all of his sticks and begins by trying to pick up one stick. The game continues until one player picks up all the sticks in one turn successfully.

*Adaptations:*

1. If you wish to prolong the game, decrease the number of sticks picked up back down to one before ending. The player able to do this first wins.

**DID YOU KNOW?** Most recreation in Laos centers around religious holidays and festivals.

**CULTURE QUEST** What are some of the holidays celebrated in Laos? How are they celebrated?

# JACKSTONES

▶ ORIGIN: **PAKISTAN**

▶ NUMBER OF PARTICIPANTS: 2 TO 4

▶ AGE: 8 AND OLDER

▶ GROSS MOTOR RATING: LOW

▶ COMPETITION LEVEL: LOW

▶ AREA: ANY

▶ EQUIPMENT: CHALK OR FLOOR TAPE

FIVE SMALL, ROUND STONES (THE JACKSTONES)

ONE MARKER FOR EACH PLAYER (COLORED STONES OR TWIGS)

**HOW TO PLAY:** Draw a circle and add the cross lines in the middle as shown here:

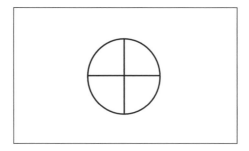

Place all personal markers on the outside rim of the circle where a line intersects. To decide which player goes first, give each player a chance to toss all five jackstones in the air at once and catch them on the backs of both hands. The person who catches the most stones goes first. Players take turns tossing the jackstones and catching them on the backs of the hands. Move the personal markers according to the following system:

- If a player catches zero stones, his marker is not moved and his turn is ended.
- If a player catches one stone, he moves his marker one finger width toward the center.
- If a player catches two stones, he moves his marker two finger widths toward the center.
- If a player catches three stones, he loses a turn and is passed over the next round.
- If a player catches four stones, he moves his marker four finger widths toward the center.
- If a player catches all five stones, he tosses them from the back of the hand to the palm, trying to catch all five stones. If he catches all five in this way, he moves the marker a full palm-width toward the center.

After each turn, the player is allowed another toss unless he caught zero or three. The player would continue until he catches zero or three even if this means several tries in a row. The player whose marker reaches the center of the circle first wins.

### *Adaptations:*
1. To make the game more difficult for more skilled players, toss and catch with one hand.
2. If you prefer, mark the cross lines with increment marks. Players move their markers the indicated number of marks instead of finger widths. This will eliminate measurement disagreements.

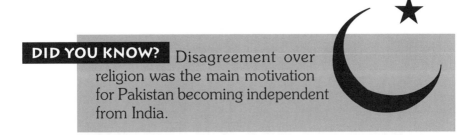

**DID YOU KNOW?** Disagreement over religion was the main motivation for Pakistan becoming independent from India.

**CULTURE QUEST** What religion are most Pakistani people?

# STICKS

▶ ORIGIN: **PAKISTAN**

▶ NUMBER OF PARTICIPANTS: 2 TO 10 FOR EACH CIRCLE

▶ AGE: 8 AND OLDER

▶ GROSS MOTOR RATING: LOW

▶ COMPETITION LEVEL: LOW

▶ AREA: ANY

▶ EQUIPMENT: CHALK OR FLOOR TAPE
SIX 1-FOOT STICKS
TWO SMALL, SOFT BALLS

**HOW TO PLAY:** Mark a circle approximately 2 feet across. Place the six round sticks randomly in the circle. Mark a throwing line 10 to 15 feet from the circle. Each player takes a turn tossing the balls at the circle, one ball at a time, attempting to knock the sticks completely out of the circle. Award five points for each stick a player knocks out of the circle. Before the next player tosses the balls, replace all the sticks in the circle. Play to a preset number of points.

*Adaptations:*

1. Players may play as individuals or in teams of two to four.

**DID YOU KNOW?** Pakistan has no law requiring children to attend school.

**CULTURE QUEST** What are the laws regarding schooling where you live?

# GAMES FROM

# AUSTRALIA

▲▲▲▲▲▲▲▲▲▲▲▲▲▲▲▲▲

# COCONUT SHELL GAME

▶ ORIGIN: **ABORIGINE**

▶ NUMBER OF PARTICIPANTS: 28

▶ AGE: 6 AND OLDER

▶ GROSS MOTOR RATING: LOW

▶ COMPETITION LEVEL: LOW

▶ AREA: ANY

▶ EQUIPMENT: 28 COCONUT HALF-SHELLS OR BEANBAGS

**HOW TO PLAY:** Divide the players into four teams of seven each, designating one player as the leader of each team. Each team forms a circle approximately 10 feet in diameter. The leader has seven coconut shells at her feet. On the signal to begin, the leader hands or tosses one shell to the player on her left. The receiving player catches the coconut shell and places it at her feet. The leader continues tossing the shells until the player on the left has all seven at her feet. Then the player with the shells tosses to the player on her left. Continue in this way until all the shells are again at the feet of the leader. The first team to return the shells to the feet of the leader wins.

*Adaptations:*

1. Play with fewer teams or a different number of players on a team. However, each team must have the same number of players.

**DID YOU KNOW?** The coconut we eat is the seed of the coconut palm tree.

**CULTURE QUEST** Make a food or drink that includes coconut as an ingredient.

# BOWLS

▶ ORIGIN: **AUSTRALIA**

▶ NUMBER OF PARTICIPANTS: 2 TO 8

▶ AGE: 6 AND OLDER

▶ GROSS MOTOR RATING: LOW

▶ COMPETITION LEVEL: LOW

▶ AREA: INDOORS OR OUTDOORS

▶ EQUIPMENT: ONE CLAY OR WOODEN BALL THAT IS NOT QUITE ROUND PER PLAYER (EACH SHOULD BE A DIFFERENT COLOR)

WHITE OR OTHER BRIGHTLY COLORED BALL (THE "JACK" BALL)

**HOW TO PLAY:** Players choose an order in which to participate. Place the white "jack" ball a distance from the starting line. Each player takes a turn rolling their ball toward the jack ball. The player owning the closest ball to the jack ball earns 1 point. If a player hits the jack ball with his ball, the player earns 3 points. All players roll a ball before any are retrieved. If a rolled ball hits another player's ball, allow both balls to land where they will. If a ball is pushed by another into the jack ball, then that ball's owner gets 3 points. When all balls have been rolled, check their positions for scoring. Play to a preset number of points, usually 11 or 21.

**DID YOU KNOW?** Australia is the only country that is also a continent.

**CULTURE QUEST** Who are the Aborigines? What was their way of life like before large numbers of British settlers arrived?

# CONTINUOUS CRICKET

▶ ORIGIN: **AUSTRALIA**

▶ NUMBER OF PARTICIPANTS: 20

▶ AGE: 12 AND OLDER

▶ GROSS MOTOR RATING: HIGH

▶ COMPETITION LEVEL: MEDIUM

▶ AREA: GRASS FIELD AT LEAST 90 FEET SQUARE

▶ EQUIPMENT: WICKET THAT IS 2.5 BY 1.5 FEET (WIRE OR WOOD)

CRICKET BAT

TENNIS BALL

CONE OR FLAG SET IN THE GROUND

MATERIAL TO MARK THE GROUND

**HOW TO PLAY:** Divide the players into two teams and arrange them in the following manner on a field at least 90 feet square:

```
    x(Catcher)                    x
       MMM(Wicket)                        </>(Flag)
    o(Batter)


ooooo              x                    x
(Batting team)
             x(Bowler's crease)


   x               x          x              x


   x = Fielding team       o = Batting team
```

One fielder stands at least 10 yards away from the batter. The line where this player stands is called the bowler's crease. The bowler (pitcher) tosses the ball underhand at the wicket from a distance of 10 to 15 yards. The ball may bounce but it does not have to. If the ball is hit by the batter, she drops the bat, runs around the flag and back, picks up the bat, and prepares to bat the next ball. If this is completed, she scores a run. At the same time, the fielders field the ball and throw it to the bowler's crease. The ball is bowled again, whether the batter is back and ready or not. If the ball misses the wicket and is not hit by the batter, the catcher returns it to the bowler's crease. The batter is out if a bowled ball hits or goes through the wicket or if a fielder catches a batted ball in the air. When a batter is out, the next batter must come up and be ready quickly. The bowler throws the ball as soon as she is ready, whether the next batter is ready or not. When all team members have been called out, the teams change sides. The team with the most runs wins. If a batter is hit by the ball because they aren't in the right position there is no impact on the game. Just pick up the ball and continue.

**DID YOU KNOW?** Cricket is one of the most popular sports in England as well as in British-influenced countries such as Australia.

**CULTURE QUEST** What sports, other than cricket, did the British bring to Australia?

# FIELDING RACE

▶ ORIGIN: **AUSTRALIA**

▶ NUMBER OF PARTICIPANTS: 10 OR MORE

▶ AGE: 9 AND OLDER

▶ GROSS MOTOR RATING: HIGH

▶ COMPETITION LEVEL: HIGH

▶ AREA: ANY LARGE AREA

▶ EQUIPMENT: ONE BALL FOR EACH TEAM
CONES TO MARK GOAL LINES

**HOW TO PLAY:** Divide the players into two teams, each team standing single file 20 to 25 feet from the goal line. Designate the first player in the line as the leader. On the signal to begin, the leader bowls his ball hard enough to cross the goal line. As soon as he releases the ball, the leader runs after it, picks it up (after it crosses the goal line), and runs back to his line. If the ball does not cross the goal line, he must bring it back and he tries again. When he reaches his team line, he hands the ball to the next player and goes to the end of the line. Continue in this fashion until the leader is in the front of the line again. The winner is the first team to have the leader in the first position holding the ball over his head.

*Adaptations:*

1. Determine the distance to the goal line based on the ability of the players.

**DID YOU KNOW?** The Great Barrier Reef, the world's largest coral reef, is located along Australia's northeast coast.

**CULTURE QUEST** Research or draw a picture of one plant or animal that lives in the Great Barrier Reef.

# LADDER JUMP

▶ ORIGIN: **AUSTRALIA**

▶ NUMBER OF PARTICIPANTS: 10 OR MORE

▶ AGE: 9 AND OLDER

▶ GROSS MOTOR RATING: LOW

▶ COMPETITION LEVEL: LOW

▶ AREA: ANY OPEN AREA

▶ EQUIPMENT: CHALK (IF PLAYING ON PAVEMENT)

**HOW TO PLAY:** Divide the players into two teams. Number the players. Player number one stands with toes on the starting line. She performs a standing broad jump forward, landing on two feet. Player number two starts with his toes on the heel marks of player one and jumps forward. If playing on pavement, you might want to draw chalk marks to show where players landed. Continue until all team members have jumped. The team that collectively jumps the greatest distance wins.

**DID YOU KNOW?** Children in remote areas of Australia attend school by two-way radio and mail.

**CULTURE QUEST** Pretend you live in Australia. What would you like and dislike about taking your schooling outside of a traditional classroom?

# HAKA -PAI
## (HAR-KAR PAY)

▶ ORIGIN: **MAORI**

▶ NUMBER OF PARTICIPANTS: 6 TO 12

▶ AGE: 9 AND OLDER

▶ GROSS MOTOR RATING: LOW

▶ COMPETITION LEVEL: LOW

▶ AREA: ANY

▶ EQUIPMENT: SMALL, SOFT BALL FOR EACH PLAYER
STRING

**HOW TO PLAY:** The Maori children played Haka-Pai with a small ball of dried flax stuffed with the down from a wild reed. The string was twisted down or fiber. The Maori children created the beat as modern children would do—with singing, clapping, or stamping.

Each player has a ball attached to a string for this rhythmic game. Players take turns clapping, singing, or stamping a song or beat. Rhythms of 6/8 time are the best for others to follow. The remainder of the players move their hands to bounce the ball lightly off their wrists to the beat. When one player has completed a song, another player provides one.

**DID YOU KNOW?** Modern-day Maoris keep the old traditions alive. For example, they greet each other by pressing their noses together.

**CULTURE QUEST** What is a common gesture of greeting where you live?

# TAPU-AE

▶ ORIGIN: **NEW ZEALAND**

▶ NUMBER OF PARTICIPANTS: 24

▶ AGE: 12 AND OLDER

▶ GROSS MOTOR RATING: HIGH

▶ COMPETITION LEVEL: HIGH

▶ AREA: GYM OR OUTDOOR

▶ EQUIPMENT: TWO PLAYGROUND BALLS OF DIFFERENT COLORS

TWO SKITTLES OR INDIAN CLUBS

**HOW TO PLAY:** Arrange the players as follows:

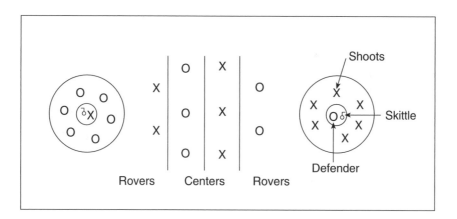

Form two teams of 12 members each. Each team has six shoots, three centers, and one defender.

The object of the game is to knock down the opponent's skittle (Indian club or pin) with a ball. A center player from each team holds a ball. On the signal to begin, she tries to throw the ball to the shoots on her team. The shoots try to knock over the skittle with the ball. Defenders protect the skittle as they and the rovers try to intercept the ball and pass it to someone on their own team. The ball must go to a center as it is being passed across to the opposite court. Both balls can be in the same circle to make it more difficult for a defender to protect her skittle.

Rules:

1. Players must stay within their own area.
2. No running with the ball allowed. Except for a step forward when throwing the ball, the player in possession of the ball must remain stationary.
3. Players must pass the ball within five seconds.
4. If a player breaks a rule, the ball goes to the closest player on the opposite team.

Scoring:

1. A player scores one point for knocking down the skittle with her team's ball.
2. A player scores two points for knocking down the skittle with the opponent's ball.
3. The first player to get 11 points wins.

### Adaptations:

1. Determine the dimensions of the playing field based upon the available playing area and the age and ability of your players.

**DID YOU KNOW?** Nearly all of New Zealand's land animals have been brought in by settlers from other countries.

**CULTURE QUEST** List five animals and birds that are native to New Zealand.

# GAME FINDER

| ORIGIN | Name of Game | Gross Motor Rating | Competition Level | Number of Players | Age | Playing Area | Equipment |
|---|---|---|---|---|---|---|---|
| Ethiopia | Spearing the Disk | L | L | 2 - 10 | 9+ | Large outdoor | Hula hoops. Small balls or sticks. |
| Ghana & Togo | Boa Constrictor | H | L | 12 - 30 | 8+ | Any large | Chalk or cones. |
| Guinea | Pebble Toss | L | L | 6 or more | 9+ | Outdoor | Small balls, nuts, or pebbles. Large food can or small pail. |
| Malawi | Kuwakha Nchuwa | L | L | 2 - 10 | 8+ | Hardtop or grass | 100-200 small, smooth pebbles. Small, round pebble. Chalk. |
| Nigeria | Abumbutan | M | L | 6 - 8 | 6+ | Outdoors or beach | Smooth stick, 8-12" long. Sandpile or pile of gravel. |
| Nigeria | Blindfolded Horse Race | H | L | 12 or more | 10+ | Any large | Blindfolds. Cones. Whistle. |
| Nigeria | Catch Your Tail | M | L | 12 or more | 6+ | Any | Handkerchiefs or cloth scraps. |
| Nigeria | Four Chiefs | H | M | 7 or more teams of 4 players each | 6+ | 50' × 100' | 4 different-colored ribbons, bands, or flags (20-30 of each color). Stopwatch. Whistle. 4 chairs, stools, or boxes. |
| Rhodesia | Poison | L | L | 8 -15 | 6+ | Any | Cloth with knot tied in middle. |
| Tanganyika | How Many? | L | L | 3 or more | 6+ | Any | Large supply of counters (pebbles, corn kernels, beads). |
| Tanganyika | My Little Bird | H | L | 20 or more | 5+ | Any | None. |

AFRICA

**EUROPE & WESTERN ASIA**

| Country | Game | | | | | | |
|---|---|---|---|---|---|---|---|
| **Belgium** | Hunter and Rabbits | H | M | 12 - 30 | 6+ | Hardtop or gym | Playground ball. |
| **Czechoslovakia** | Nations | M | L | 6 - 15 | 10+ | Any circular area about 20' across | Material to mark the field. Volleyball-size soft ball. |
| **Denmark** | Danish Rounders | M | M | 8 - 20 | 12+ | Tennis court | Tennis ball. Chalk to mark court. Wiffle ball bat or tennis racket. |
| **Eastern Europe** | Dreidel Game | L | L | 2 - 10 | 6+ | Any | 4-sided top with stem (dreidel). Paint and paintbrush. Beads or candies. |
| **England** | Corkscrew | M | L | 8 - 40 | 10+ | Any | 2-4 cones or chairs. Whistle. |
| **England** | Hopscotch | L | L | 2 - 6 | 5+ | Hardtop | Chalk or floor tape. Flat stone or other marker. |
| **England** | Human Skittles | H | L | 3 | 10+ | Any | Material to mark playing surface. Soccer or playground ball. |
| **England** | Round Hopscotch | L | L | 2 - 6 | 5+ | Hardtop | Chalk or floor tape. Small, smooth stone or other marker. |
| **Germany** | German Hopscotch | L | L | 2 - 6 | 5+ | Hardtop | Chalk or floor tape. Small, flat stone or other marker. |
| **Germany** | Schlagball | M | M | 12 or more | 12+ | Open | Softball-size rubber playground ball. Cone or base. Baseball bat. |
| **Greece** | Greek Ball Game | M | M | 20 - 30 | 9+ | Any large | Playground ball or volleyball. Whistle. Material to mark the playing field. |

| ORIGIN | Name of Game | Gross Motor Rating | Competition Level | Number of Players | Age | Playing Area | Equipment |
|---|---|---|---|---|---|---|---|
| **Greece** | Skyros | H | M | 20 - 30 | 10+ | Hardtop or grass | Playground ball or volleyball. Tape or chalk to mark court. Whistle. Pinnies or colored T-shirts. |
| **Greece** | Triangle Game | L | L | 2 - 6 | 6+ | Hardtop | Chalk. Small, colored stones or other markers. |
| **Italy** | Gioco del Mondo | L | L | 2 - 6 | 6+ | Pavement or floor | Chalk or floor tape. Small, smooth stone or other marker. |
| **Luxembourg** | Pepperches | M | L | 5 - 10 | 8+ | Any area with a wall | Small, soft rubber ball. |
| **Russia** | Goellki | L | L | 11 - 41 (odd number) | 8+ | Any | None. |
| **Russia** | Ribaki | M | L | 5 - 20 | 5+ | Any | Heavy string. Corrugated cardboard cut in fish shapes. Crayons or felt markers. Hole puncher. Scissors. |
| **Russia** | Square Pull | H | M-H | 40 - 80 | 8+ | Any large | 2 lengths of heavy rope 20-30 feet long. Whistle. 4 cones. |
| **Switzerland** | Hallihallo | L | L | 10 or more | 9+ | Any | Soft rubber ball or beanbag. |
| **Argentina** | Balon en el Aire | H | L | 30 - 40 | 10+ | Gym or grass | Volleyball or playground ball. Cones or material to mark field. Whistle. Pen and paper. |

**EUROPE & WESTERN ASIA**

| Region | Country | Game | | | Players | Age | Space | Equipment |
|---|---|---|---|---|---|---|---|---|
| CENTRAL & SOUTH AMERICA | Brazil | Peteca | M | L | Any | 8+ | Any | Peteca or badminton shuttlecock. |
| | Chile | Chueca | H | H | 20 or more | 12+ | Hardtop or gym | Hockey sticks. Rubber hockey ball. Pinnies or colored T-shirts. |
| | Chile-Arauco Province Indians | El Pullmatun | H | M | 4 - 30 | 8+ | Outdoor or gym | Long rope (about 100'). Small playground ball. |
| | Colombia | Cintas de Colores | L | L | 10 - 30 | 8+ | Any | None. |
| | Guatemala | O.A. | H | L | 5 | 5+ | Smooth with wall | 5 tennis balls or small playground balls. |
| | Mexico | Bolan Maldecida | M | L | Any number of pairs | 9+ | Any open | Small, soft foam ball. |
| | Peru | Bola | L | L | 4 - 10 | 8+ | Hardtop or gym | Bowling ball-size rubber ball. 3 Indian clubs or bowling pins. |
| | Peru | Reloj | M | L | 4 - 20 | 6+ | Any with high ceiling | Long jump rope. |
| | Puerto Rico | El Gato y el Raton | L | L | 10 - 30 | 5+ | Any open | None. |
| NORTH AMERICA | Alaska | Ha-Goo | H | M | 20 or more | 9+ | Any | Brightly colored banner on a stick. |
| | Alaska | Musk Oxen | H | M | 12 or more | 9+ | Any | 4-6 sponge balls or blunt arrows. Squares of fabric. |
| | Hawaii | Bowling the Maika Stone | M | M | 2 - 6 | 12+ | Smooth, flat | Flat, round stones or round, wooden "stones" about 6 inches. 2 cones or sticks to mark goal. |

| ORIGIN | Name of Game | Gross Motor Rating | Competition Level | Number of Players | Age | Playing Area | Equipment |
|---|---|---|---|---|---|---|---|
| North American Indian | Bas-Quoits | L | L | 2 - 4 | 10+ | Grass | 2 16"-18" wooden pegs. 4 4"-5" rope rings, painted. Hammer. |
| North American Indian | Battledore and Shuttlecock | L | L | 4 - 12 | 12+ | Any | Homemade shuttlecocks and battledores or badminton shuttlecocks and ping-pong paddles. |
| North American Zuni Indian | Clown Game | H | H | 20 or more | 12+ | Any large | Homemade rawhide balls or small, soft balls. Strong cord. Cones or goals. |
| North American Pueblo Indian | Dodge Ball | M | M | 10 - 30 | 9+ | Gym or outdoor | Soft homemade ball or soft rubber ball. |
| North American Blackfoot Indian | Hands and Bones | L | L | 2 - 12 | 8+ | Any | 1 stick 6" long with a black ring painted on it. 1 plain stick 6" long. |
| North American Indian | Indian Wrestling | H | H | Any number of pairs | 9+ | Any | None. |
| North American Choctaw Indian | Stealing Sticks | H | M | 2 - 30 | 6+ | Large outdoor | 10-12 18" sticks. Material for marking field. Whistle. |

NORTH AMERICA

| Region | Country | Game |  |  | Players | Age | Space | Materials |
|---|---|---|---|---|---|---|---|---|
| NORTH AMERICA | North American Indian | Turn Around Game | H | M | 2 - 8 in partners | 12+ | Any | 20-40 6" sticks for each pair of partners. |
| | United States | Skelly | L | L | 2 - 6 | 6+ | Pavement or gym | Smooth stone, coin-size wooden piece, or bottle cap filled with wax for each player. |
| | United States | Steal the Bacon | L | L | 20 - 30 | 7+ | Any large | Indian club or plastic bowling pin. |
| EAST ASIA | Burma | Loo K'Bah Zee | M | L | 12 or more | 6+ | Any | Small ball or beanbag. |
| | Ceylon | Train Stations | L | L | 10 - 30 | 10+ | Any | None. |
| | China | Catching Fishes in the Dark | M | L | 8 - 20 | 5+ | Any | Blindfold. |
| | China | Chinese Chicken | M | L | 10 - 20 | 9+ | Any | Shoes, wooden blocks, or beanbags. |
| | China | Chinese Wall | H | L | 10 - 50 | 6+ | Any | Material to mark playing surface. |
| | Hong Kong | Plant Beans, Reap Beans | M | L | 8 - 20 | 6+ | Any large | 10 "beans" (checkers). Chalk. Whistle. |
| | India | Atya-Patya | H | L | 10 - 20 | 9+ | Tennis court or gym with lines | Chalk or floor tape. Stopwatch. Whistle. |
| | Indonesia | Foot Game | L | L | 2 or more | 8+ | Outdoor | Small, smooth stones. |
| | Indonesia | Ring and Loose Rope Game | L | L | 10 - 30 | 6+ | Any | Heavy string. Plastic or wooden ring (curtain ring). |
| | Japan | Big Lantern | L | L | 10 or more | 6+ | Any | None. |
| | Japan | Bounce the Ball | L | L | 2 - 10 | 8+ | Hardtop | Playground ball. |

| ORIGIN | Name of Game | Gross Motor Rating | Competition Level | Number of Players | Age | Playing Area | Equipment |
|---|---|---|---|---|---|---|---|
| **Japan** | Japanese Tag | H | L | 10 - 30 | 8+ | Any large | None. |
| Laos | Pick-Up Sticks | L | L | 2 - 4 | 5+ | Any level | 15-30 10" chopsticks or similar sticks. Small ball or large nut. |
| **Pakistan** | Jackstones | L | L | 2 - 4 | 8+ | Any | Chalk or floor tape. 5 small, round stones. 2-4 markers. |
| **Pakistan** | Sticks | L | L | 2 - 10 (per circle) | 8+ | Any | Chalk or floor tape. 6 1' sticks. 2 small, soft balls. |
| **Aborigine** | Coconut Shell Game | L | L | 28 | 6+ | Any | 28 coconut shell halves or beanbags. |
| **Australia** | Bowls | L | L | 2 - 8 | 6+ | Any | 1 clay or wooden ball that is not quite round per player. White or other brightly colored ball. |
| **Australia** | Continuous Cricket | H | M | 20 | 12+ | Grassy field | Wicket. Cricket bat. Tennis ball. Cone or flag. Material to mark field. |
| **Australia** | Fielding Race | H | H | 10 or more | 9+ | Any large | Ball for each team. Cones to mark goal lines. |
| **Australia** | Ladder Jump | L | L | 10 or more | 9+ | Any open | Chalk (if playing on pavement). |
| **Maori** | Haka-Pai | L | L | 6 - 12 | 9+ | Any | Small, soft ball for each player. String. |
| **New Zealand** | Tapu-Ae | H | H | 24 | 12+ | Gym or outdoor | 2 playground balls of different colors. 2 skittles or Indian clubs. |

EAST ASIA

AUSTRALIA

# REFERENCES

1. Brewster, Paul G. 1953. *American nonsinging games.* Norman, OK: University of Oklahoma Press.

2. International Council of Health, Physical Education and Recreation. 1967. *Book of worldwide games and dances.* Washington, DC: American Association for Health, Physical Education and Recreation.

3. Hunt, Sarah E. 1964. *Games and sports the world around.* 3d ed. New York: Ronald Press.

4. Millen, Nina. 1965. *Children's games from many lands.* New York: Friendship Press.

5. National Association for Sport and Physical Education. 1995. *Moving into the future: National standards for physical education.* St. Louis: Mosby.

# ABOUT THE AUTHOR

Lorraine Barbarash has been teaching in a multiethnic high school in New York since 1978 and has been the assistant principal for health and physical education and the athletic director there since 1987. Her extensive experience working with children also includes more than three decades at camps as a counselor, group leader, athletic director, and assistant head counselor; several seasons as a varsity, high-school girl's and boy's soccer coach; and three years as a Cub Scout den leader.

Lorraine is also the author of *Are We Having Fun Yet?*, a popular games and activity book that was listed as a best-seller by the American Camping Association for two years. She has presented workshops based on the book at the American Camping Association Conference.

A member of the American Association of Health, Physical Education, Recreation and Dance and the National Soccer Coaches Association of America, Lorraine holds a master's degree in supervision and administration in health and physical education. She lives in Staten Island, New York, where she enjoys reading, walking, and attending her son's athletic games.